One Woman's Miracle: Everyone's Journey

My Amazing Journey from Death Back to Life

SYLVIA L. MARTIN

ONE WOMAN'S MIRACLE: EVERYONE'S JOURNEY
© Sylvia L. Martin 2013

Sylvia L. Martin has asserted her rights under the Copyright Designs and Patents Act 1988 to be identified as the author of this work.

All rights reserved. No part of this book may be used or reproduced in any manner whatsoever, including Internet usage, without the written permission of Sylvia Martin , except in the case of brief quotations embodied in critical articles and reviews.

National Library of Australia Cataloguing-in-Publication entry (pbk)

Creator: Martin, Sylvia L., author.

Title:	One Woman's Miracle: Everyone's Journey / Sylvia L. Martin
ISBN:	9781925388367 (paperback)
Subjects:	Martin, Sylvia L. Near-death experiences. Life change events. Self-consciousness. Self-actualization (Psychology).

Dewey Number: 133.9013

Published by InHouse Publishing
www.inhousepublishing.com.au

About the Author

Sylvia Martin was born in Sydney, Australia, in 1937. After World War Two and her father Jack's discharge from the Australian Army, the family moved to Wollongong where she was educated and started her career in nursing at just seventeen years old. It was in Wollongong that she also married her husband Michael, who worked for the New South Wales Police Force, rising to the rank of detective in the Criminal Investigation Division.

After their four children left home, Sylvia and Michael moved to the Sunshine Coast in Queensland to retire. Sylvia has been a widow for many years now and after her Near Death Experience in 2005, she has given many talks on her amazing journey. In this, her first book, she relates these events and wishes to share with you the knowledge to realise Who You Really Are and What Your Purpose in Life is really all about.

You can contact Sylvia via email at:
sylvialornamartin@gmail.com

Readers' Responses to One Woman's Miracle, Everyone's Journey

"This world is perfect, but then you have to understand what perfection is as far as the Universe is concerned, not your own idealism, which is usually created from your own belief systems and teachings. This book will help you understand how right the experience you are now living is perfect in every single one of us. How could it not be! Oh! Do not let me hear you say 'then you must not have suffered' for it is usually the opposite that is the case. For when your suffering (emotional pain) reaches a certain point, you have the chance to turn your idealism into perfection. When this transformation takes place, I say your understanding will become like the tide. Try making the tide come in, when it is not, but once you wake up, try stopping it when it does."

—Mark Bootle, Mudjimba

"I highly recommend this amazing book. It will be a shining light in your time of need. When I read it, it was like I was going on a personal journey of self-discovery."

—Gwen Hodder, Point Arkwright,
Spiritual Counsellor and
Hypnotherapy Practitioner

"One woman's inspiring journey from adversity to 'The Other Side' and back, to share her knowledge and wisdom."
—Sandi A. Buderim

"Sylvia is a very special friend, I have known her for many years and she has so much love to give and helps many people to move on. She is amazing for what she has gone through. This is a wonderful story."
—Jenny Burns, Eumundi

"Sylvia Martin is a survivor, no matter what the challenge, she deals with it. She comes through with a smile on her face. When she was critically ill, the doctors said they could do no more, however, she proved that the Spirit is stronger than the body and fought her way back; a superhuman effort. She is serene and kind, nothing is too much trouble, she is always there for those who need her, it is a pleasure and privilege to be her friend and this book will help many in need of direction."
—Kaye Perrett, Yass

Dedication

*I dedicate this book to my fellow Earth Travellers
who are seeking higher knowledge.
To Who They Really Are in their quest for happiness,
inner peace and understanding of
this third dimension we call Earth.
Never deviate from your passion
for you can achieve it all.*

Preface

Sometimes in life, things are just meant to be. After my Near Death Experience in May 2005, I experienced ten months in hospital over a period of seventeen months and an additional couple of years recovering from the ordeal. During the operation my bowel was accidentally cut.

I knew I needed to write about all the experiences I had during this time, both Earthly and spiritually, but my health was so fragile for so long, the thought of it all was just too much to think about at the time.

Many friends and family members would say to me, "You have to write a book about all these things" and I would reply, "Yes I will, when the time is right."

Well, years went by and one morning at 4 am on the 2nd of February 2013, I woke up with a voice in my ear saying to me, "Time to write your book." I hopped out of bed, grabbed a pad and pen, sat down and started my book. Going back over my childhood, I wrote for over two hours, then the feeling faded, so I put the pad away.

Three days later, the huge urge came again, so after many more hours of writing, this book came into being. However, I only wrote when that energy came within me.

It has been the most wonderful experience writing about my life. I would recommend it to everyone. Just going through all the different phases of life and letting go of so many things that really are quite irrelevant is truly cleansing and helps remove any emotional cobwebs from our psyche.

Contents

	Introduction My Amazing Journey.	1
I	Wake up! You are so Much More Than you Think.	3
II	Compassion is Helping Others Without Detriment to Self.	9
III	Being in Your Power is True Love of One's Self.	15
IV	Love and Fear Cannot Exist in the Same Time Space.	35
V	Don't Try to Make Someone Else's Life Your Own.	41
VI	Love Cannot be Found Until you are Found.	47
VII	Every Human who has Left a Footprint on Earth is a Hero.	53
VIII	As I began to love myself, I found that anguish, and emotional suffering are only warning signs that I was living against my truth.	59
IX	Love is Like the Wind, you Cannot See it, but you Know That it's There.	63
X	Have you Ever Asked Yourself, "What is my Purpose in Life"?	77

XI	When Your Inner Self Becomes Your Outer Self, Your Outer Self is Everywhere.	87
XII	You are the Silence Between Your Thoughts.	95
XIII	Do You Want to be Powerful or Powerless?	101
XIV	Have You Ever Asked Yourself: Who Am I?	107
XV	Have you Ever Asked Yourself: Why am I Here?	113

Glossary of Terms: 133
Bibliography 135
Acknowledgments 137

Introduction
My Amazing Journey

This is the story of my life; of how I was a work-in-progress from an early age and the amazing journey I took to find myself and in doing so wake up to Who I Really Am. This story spans decades of emotional heartfelt pain and is about my struggle of letting go of the conditionings of this world and of this dimension. This book is about how nearing the latter part of my life, I had the most amazing experience of all, an experience of death and what I learned from that. This experience completely changed me and the way I look at life; it put all the missing pieces of the puzzle of life together.

It is my hope that you enjoy reading this book. True, you may find parts of it controversial, but perhaps it may also awaken in you something for which you have long been searching.

From the first time you open your eyes in this lifetime, to the last time you shut them in this lifetime, the only thing that can happen to you in this life is a continual flow of events that is within the human experience. Once you understand it is the "Isness" of life and the *circumstances* of life and you refuse to pay the experiences of life with emotional pain, there is no price to pay.

It is just the "Isness" of life.

1
Wake up! You are so Much More Than you Think

May I share with you a journey, one that had no apparent hope and even led to death, but out of which came trust, acceptance, understanding, inner peace and life.

As I look back on my life in a reflective state of being, I can see how we come full circle. From *birth to death*, sometimes things happen in a cycle that does not always go to plan.

As a young woman growing up and also throughout my childhood, I really did not have an inkling of what lay ahead in my life's latter stages; events that would lift me entirely out of my conditioning of how life was meant to be. Sure, I was taught like everyone else that this is the way we conduct ourselves in this world. Growing up, we were taught to have good manners, respect for elders and to never question why. Just do what you were told, never answer back; children were to be seen but not heard. Remember, I was born in 1937, near the end of the Great Depression and I didn't know any better than what I was told. Namely, never to question authority! What a different world it was back then compared to what it is today.

As a child, I had many strange experiences, like finding myself at the very early age out in the backyard in the middle of the night, knowing I had been somewhere with different people—but I couldn't remember where. I just knew that I always felt safe and loved by these other people. My family put it all down to sleep walking, but I used to tell my mother Sylvia, whom I was named after, that I had another family somewhere else. I was always asking her if I was adopted.

One night, when I was around five years old, my mother was taking me to the toilet which was in the backyard in those days and we had just lost our much loved cocker spaniel, Jilliwinks. We were all very sad about it and just as we walked up the path that night, there on the grass in front of us, in a bluish white hazy light, was Jilly. We went up to her and patted her and she felt like wet velvet; then she just disappeared.

I also remember the search lights in the sky at night and all the windows blacked out when we lived in a suburb of Sydney during the Second World War. There was a boundary rider on a horse going from house to house of a night to make sure there were no lights to be seen. My mother was a warden and had had her turn of duty going around the streets as well, to check on any lights. She had a tin hat and a haversack with a gas mask in it. During these years of war, my brothers and I knew a war was happening far away, but didn't really have a concept of what was really going on. Our mother read all the letters from our father Jack to us and he would write on the top of them all the places he had been to on all fronts of the war. We all hoped and prayed he would come home safely to us.

My father was in the army, as were most of the men around us, so neither my two brothers Bill and John, or myself, the baby of the family, saw our father for six years. I look back on those years and think how hard it must have been for our mother, especially in moments like when she received a telegram from the war department saying our father was missing, presumed dead after the taking of Crete. It was a truly devastating time. Everyone rallied around us, but as I was only around four at the time, I didn't really understand the significance of it all. I knew I had a father somewhere, but didn't really remember him.

My mother was terribly upset and traumatised by this telegram, so my Aunty Elsie came to stay with us to comfort her. That night, I was awakened by a beautiful lady standing by my bed. She smiled at me and told me my father was not with them and not to be sad. I woke my mother and told her what had happened, she kissed and hugged me so tightly to her and said in such a tender voice that I had had a lovely dream and we would pray for my dream to come true; but it was so real to me.

Just a few days later, new neighbours moved in. They were lovely people who went on to become lifetime friends. What came next, I remember so well but l need to tell it in my mother's words.

Uncle Eric, as we called him, along with Aunty Ena, came over for a welcome-to-the-neighbourhood cup of tea. My mother showed him the telegram. He took off his glasses and held the telegram and went into a deep trance and began talking to someone unseen in a foreign language. He then said to my mother, "This one is not with us, he is still on the Earth plane, you will receive communication about him in nine moons (months); he will be found where the palm trees sway." Of course, my mother and all of us were so excited about this strange happening. Mum told my uncle what I had said about my lovely lady and he replied that I had a predestined future to fulfil, which would unfold as I grew up. He said it would be a life with many hardships and emotionally draining things to learn and overcome, but that the latter part of my life would see me conquering it all. What's more, I would have a full understanding of why I was here on this earth.

How absolutely true all his words were. This is the reason why I have written this book to help others to wake up and realise that the worst adversities in our lives are the greatest gifts to help us understand. To help us learn and discern Who We Really Are and Why We Are Here in this third dimension. Why we have our individual experiences and our choices in how we deal with them is how we take control of our own destiny.

The wonderful news about our father brought much needed happiness to our daily lives, especially to our mother. Every Saturday night a séance was held in our lounge room and through Uncle Eric we kept track of our father. Nine months later, Mum received a telegram from the Red Cross saying our father had been found in a Scottish hospital in Lebanon. To this very day, I still have those telegrams. My dad had been rescued after spending days in the sea, marooned and striving to stay afloat off Crete, a wallet with our photos in it clamped in his teeth. How lucky he was to have been a good swimmer, as he had been a life saver at Byron Bay Surf Club in his youth. He clung to the hope that there was another chapter of his life yet to be written and told us many years later how we were never out of his thoughts and how he longed to get home to us.

Rescued by the local people, Dad was taken up the mountain and with their help, was finally found in Lebanon.

For my mother, this experience was also a journey. She herself soon became a wonderful trance medium and it just took meeting the right people to bring out her own psychic abilities, though of course the time was right as well. I have found everything that happens to us has to happen at the right time in order for it to be understood.

II
Compassion is Helping Others Without Detriment to Self

—Mark Bootle

So many things happened surrounding my father, Jack, after being wounded on the Kokoda Trail in New Guinea near the end of the war. Even though he was being sent home, our friends on the other side told my mother she would not see him for six months.

This was another forecast that turned out to be true, as he was off-loaded to a hospital in Perth with an infected leg wound and severe dermatitis. Once we had word he was coming home—after six months in hospital—my brothers and I went to the train station to meet him. There were so many soldiers, sailors and air force men and among the crowd we could not find Dad. We went home and found him there; we had passed him as he had passed us, as we didn't know each other. We hadn't seen him for six years!

Well, what a different life it was with a father back in the home. He would whistle at us when we were out playing and if we didn't immediately come home, no play the next day. Such a thing was a great shock to our systems and way of life. We were certainly good kids, but were used to the softer love of our mother. Looking back, I probably felt resentment that he had come back into our lives, as I was then smartly put into place in my own room—whereas before he came home, I had always slept with my mother.

He was very hard on my two brothers, especially Bill. Yet our mother thought the sun and the moon shone out of my father and continued to do so for the rest of her life. This is probably why I could never tell her what happened to me. I was two when he went to war and eight when he came back and he started sexually abusing me only months after he returned. I was frightened of him, but I could not tell my mother; she was so happy to have him back. I kept this period of time from age eight to fourteen to myself; in fact, until I was sixty-five years old. What I have to tell you in the coming pages was the last thing I had to deal with to release me from my self-imprisonment, brought about by my father. I knew I had to do something about my big black secret, as I kept slamming the door in my mind every time it reared its ugly head.

At age sixty-five, I went to see two dear friends, Mark and Pam, who are wonderful healers with their own method of releasing emotional pain and entities. I plucked up my courage and confided to them, "I'm ready to deal with this issue. It is a constant in my head and I want to let it go." Mark asked, after he explained certain things to me, "What happened to you when you were eight?" I just came out with it, "My father raped me." I couldn't believe I had said it, but when I did, I had this huge emotional release.

When I stood up from the healing table that morning I felt free, wonderful, enlightened and so happy. So often, we do not realise what releasing our deepest guilt and worries does for our body. It enlightens our cellular structure; it enlightens and frees us. We hold this emotional pain within us for years, eating away at us and this is what brings on our illnesses.

That same night, I had a dream; only it was real. My father was before me; he had passed away at fifty-nine years of age. A table was between us and then two spiritual guides brought a scroll and unrolled it for us to see. It was a scroll about my life and while it was all in symbols, I could read it and understand it. I could see why the sexual abuse had happened, as I knew we could not take just this life into consideration; many lives are involved in our being Who We Are. This is because if something that has happened in a previous life is not understood and resolved, it will follow us through to all future lives in our DNA genetic line; until it is resolved. All must be put into balance, the Universe itself must be in balance and this life was the one where I finally resolved this energetic pattern that had followed me for many lifetimes. I had now resolved the negative energy surrounding that circumstance—and now all was put back into balance.

I looked at my dad, then went to him and put my arms around him. In that very moment with him there I said, "I love you; I understand," for I saw in that scroll that I had been part of it too, in other lifetimes where I wasn't the innocent one. In response to me in that time and space, my father said, "That's wonderful, now we can both get on with our lives. I love you."

I now only think of my father with love, as at fourteen years of age, I had finally gained the courage to say "No," and then kept my distance from him.

What a momentous time this was to realise I had been holding that resentment, fear and guilt for all those years. I had let it colour my whole life about men. My inner self-confidence and self-esteem had been whittled away; I had punished myself over something that had happened to me when I was a little girl and had lived in fear all those years. For me, that moment was a new beginning. Hard fought and painfully won, but a new beginning all the same.

I realised I couldn't change what had happened, but I could certainly change the way I felt about it. I made the choice to accept what had happened and to get on with my life. A huge big part of me that was once so dark is now filled with love. When

I reflect back to that time with my Dad, my heart is open and filled with love for him. I now have a much better understanding of not only my, but everybody's experiences and how we all learn and grow from the understanding of our choices, which can bring our emotions back into balance and stop the blame game. Why should we go through emotional suffering all our lives when we can resolve these issues much easier than we sometimes think!

III

Being in Your Power is True Love of One's Self

—Mark Bootle

So much had happened in the interim. I look back and think, my goodness, I have led at least six lifetimes in one. I realised I was finishing off all the bits and pieces I hadn't dealt with in the many years and decades of my past and present lives. I was understanding and realising what life was really all about, looking at an issue, taking responsibility for my part in it and making the choice of letting it go. I was learning not to care. I was *waking up*!

While I was growing up, I could read people—how they really felt, whether they were telling the truth or not—I could see behind their public face and see when the truth wasn't being told. This made me feel very uncomfortable at first and I wondered why others couldn't feel or see as I did. I was quite intuitive about many things and sometimes friends would think I was quite strange. My mother used to say to me, "You have a special gift, don't let it worry you." I used to hide a lot of what I saw and felt and kept it under wraps. Hey, I wanted to be normal like the other kids, although really I knew I wasn't. Apart from my gift, I had a big dark secret about my father.

A week after my seventeenth birthday I started nursing as that was what I had always wanted to do. I loved it, it was like second nature to me. I knew things before they were told to me and I had this huge well of compassion wanting to pour itself over every patient I nursed, or over the people I came into contact with. It seems I was born with this feeling of caring for animals and people; it is still with me to this day.

Since I was about ten years old, I used to go and help my mother's younger sister, Aunty Mavis, with her five children—all five years and under. Her husband, Keith, was killed in a car accident when the youngest, Tommy, was two months old. I quickly became used to handling babies and little ones. I did this for many years, until my cousin Mavis came to stay with Aunty Mavis and I began nursing. She was a lovely aunt and I still think of her with so much love.

Many years later I nursed my mother for three months with cancer of the throat and watched my lovely spiritual mother choking to death, watched her accept her coming death in such a beautiful and understanding way. I was completely devastated. Six months after her death she came to me with my Aunty Mavis, who had passed away a year before and there they were, standing by my bed smiling down on me, both young and happy. What a wonderful moment it was. My mother said to me, "Do not grieve and be unhappy, I am so happy here, enjoy your life my precious girl, there is so much awaiting you." This was a precious time as I was in a very unhappy state of mind. My husband Michael was a very difficult, domineering man and we were not in a very happy marriage. It is so true about the laws of attraction; my experience with my father attracted me to a very similar sort of man, a very controlling man.

During the time I looked after my mother before her death, my husband did not come down once to Woy Woy, New South Wales, in that three months to see me or my mother. I understood in a way, as he was not really well himself with heart trouble, but he could have made the effort as this was such a heart-wrenching time for both my mother and I. My daughter, Jennifer, came and helped me when she could, as she was then nursing in Sydney. Sadly, Michael seemed to lack empathy around issues not concerning himself.

After my mother's estate had been dealt with and the house put up for sale and as I kissed and waved goodbye to my two brothers, Bill and John, I got into the car to leave my mother's house for the last time. My heart just burst open with sadness, but also with so many happy memories of the times we had spent together. It felt like a huge chapter of my life was closing and the thought of not seeing my mother again made the tears roll down my cheeks and I couldn't leave or start the car on that final journey for quite a while, as memories of her kept flashing in my mind.

It was a very long drive from Sydney to north of Brisbane, so I stopped for a night at a friend's place; at Elma and Con's beautiful home at Kempsey where I was made so welcome and looked after so well. It was just what I needed at that time. I then carried on early the next morning, only to hit pouring rain which lasted all the way home. Michael had said to stop another night somewhere as it was still a long way to go, but I kept driving until I reached the Gold Coast late in the afternoon. I was exhausted and quite down from all the happenings of the last three months and I just wanted to get home.

I arrived at about 8.30pm that night; I grabbed my handbag and raced to the front door as it was still pouring with rain. I pressed the doorbell for Michael to let me in. He came to the door—are you picturing a lovely welcome home? No way, my welcome was him looking at me and asking, "What the bloody hell are you doing here? I told you to stay another night somewhere." He was hostile towards me. I thought to myself, *Why did I think he'd be any different?* I pushed past him, tripping over countless pairs of shoes just inside the front door and said, "I just wanted to get home, God knows why, thanks for the nice welcome!" He ranted and raved at me and then said, "We're getting visitors for Christmas." I said, "No, I can't do that, I'm exhausted, I need some time out, I can't do it, there's nothing prepared, the house is a mess and it's five days to Christmas." He replied, "Well that's too bad, they're coming." I looked at him and stated, "Okay, you can look after them." My reaction to him was picking up a shoe out of my frustration and throwing it at him, which shocked him, but spurred me on to throw the rest of the shoes at him as he ran up the hallway calling out to me, "You're bloody mad" and I screamed back at him, "I know I am and you made me like it, you insensitive bastard." How could a man that professed to love me treat me like this, especially under the circumstances?

I made myself a cup of tea, had a shower and went to bed. If he had just given me a hug, it would have made everything alright, but he didn't even do that. He was angry I had spent that time looking after my dying mother. This was the start of the finish of how I really felt about him. He seemed to take the greatest pleasure in seeing me upset and I could see the triumph in his face when he thought he had achieved that. I thought to myself, *Is this the same lovely young man I fell in love with? I wonder what happened to him?*

I had quite a lot to work out in my mind about things, remember I wasn't awake as I am now about life, but was quickly learning. The morning after I came home I just knew I had to get away from him. I had heard about Chenrezig, but didn't know a thing about it, only that it was a Buddhist Monastery up in the mountains near Eudlo on the Sunshine Coast. So early the next morning, while Michael was out in his garden, I looked up the number, rang them and asked if I could go up there and stay for a while. They said, "Yes" and explained to me how to get there.

I packed a few clothes; everything else was still in the car and walked out the front door to go. Michael said to me, "Where do you think you're going?" I answered, "As far away from you as possible! I'm going to Eudlo to the Buddhist Monastery to get myself together, otherwise I'll go back in the kitchen and get that big knife and stick it in your gut." He must have seen something in me, as he just stood there as I drove away. Perhaps I had touched some deep seated compassion within him, as there was a look of shock on his face. I felt so good about what I had just said to him and I thought, *Hey, who bloody cares,* so I turned up the music in my car and off I went to Chenrezig.

I stayed there over Christmas and New Year; three weeks in all and met some lovely people from all over Australia and other countries. I joined in the meditations, took lovely walks and just spent time on

Me. The Buddhist nuns welcomed me with open arms and I felt safe and nurtured with wonderful vegan food. I joined in a Lamrim course, meaning Your Pathway in Buddhism and that was over a period of ten days. This brought me inner peace and tranquillity. I had some heartfelt talks with the nuns, who were really quite wonderful and made me understand not to meet aggression with aggression.

I returned home in a completely different state of mind, accepting Michael at that time and how things were. I knew I couldn't change him, but only myself and how I looked at things; being accepting and understanding while having the choice of what I wanted to do about things. Michael was different for a little while, but soon was back to his old self and I also slipped back into some of my old conditioning for a while as well.

As I write this and remember it all so well after all those years with him gone, I remember he said when I came home, "How was your time in the mountains with the kooks?" At least he was consistent.

After all these years, I can see how I have grown so much in my acceptance and understanding of this circumstance and really have to laugh at my knife threat as it was so unlike me; but it did make him sit up and take notice. Now it all seems like it happened to someone else in another life, as it is currently so remote from me.

I first met Michael when I was about fourteen years old and used to ride my bicycle everywhere with my friend Marjie. We would ride to tennis, sports days, basically everywhere—as did all the kids in those days. Marjie and I used to stop and talk to Michael as we passed each other on our bikes; then I didn't see him for a few years until I started nursing. I was at a hospital ball and there he was with another policeman at the front entrance of the ballroom. I thought to myself, *Oh, that's Michael*. He looked so dashing and handsome standing there in his uniform. He looked over and winked at me and my heart gave a little flutter. I didn't know he had joined the police force, but there he was and he also turned up at our next hospital dance, as these were held once a month. I said to him, "What are you doing here?" and he answered, "I came to see you."

We started going out. I was nineteen by this time and madly in love. I became pregnant, we married and that ended my nursing career and thus began the toughest test of my life. I look back and realise I was looking for someone to love me, as I didn't love myself and felt very insecure. Little did I know what I was in for over the next forty years, as with so many people, they show the public face of themselves, but eventually the real self makes its appearance and that's how it was with Michael.

I didn't see his real self at the time in him, or didn't want to. Gradually my friends dropped away; he hated me going anywhere and was very controlling. I was so naive, always trying to please him; but somehow I never could. Over all those years, I never did anything right in his eyes; he was so critical and silly me let him eat away my self-confidence and my self-esteem. It took me years to realise I was letting him do this to me. I was allowing this to happen; I let myself become the victim—poor me.

I was in my forties and after my three boys were married and Jennifer had started nursing, I finally started to take more of my power back. I had had enough. I said to myself, "I am not going to take this anymore" and I didn't. I had said this before, but somehow would fall back into the old patterns.

At a great shock to Michael, I would go where I pleased. I still copped all the verbal abuse, but I didn't care as by this time most of my feelings for him had gone and I felt a huge resentment towards him. The only time he had been physically abusive towards me was when I was seven months pregnant with my youngest son and I told him I knew he was having another affair. In a drunken rage, he choked me up against a wall. I left him and took the children home to my mother's until after I had had the baby. It was with a very heavy heart that I went back as three little children in a small house with a father on different time duties was just too much. It wasn't fair to them. So I went back home as it was the easiest solution to a very hard decision. In those days there was no outside help. This was a great learning curve and I chose to go back mainly for the children, so I accepted that and just got on with life and tried to make the best I could out of the situation.

It felt like everything happened in just a few blinks of the eye, but looking back I'd had three boys in four years, so barefoot and pregnant really applied to me. In all that time I thought I could change him--how naive was that! I look back on those years and just shake my head of how asleep I was.

Eight years later, I had Jennifer, a great joy in our lives; the boys loved her and used to fight over who would take her for walks. I led quite a lonely meagre existence; me at home with the children which of course suited Michael fine—while he did whatever he wished. It was me who took the children to all their school events and sports; I love my children and I used to think to myself, *These kids are going to have one good parent*, as I was always there for them.

I started playing tennis with neighbours when Graham was about four at a ladies' social club nearby. Michael wouldn't talk to me for days. I had done something out of his control. This, of course, was to make me feel guilty and give it up, but I didn't; it was like a bit of freedom. My life was truly Hell, but I was starting to realise this and wake up more. I had let myself be a victim; let him do this to me. I started letting go of my old conditioning of always being the good, obedient wife who was taking on all this guilt over just wanting a bit of life. I began to stand up to his bullying ways and was starting to take my power back—and it felt good. I was accused of having affairs if I went to tennis, or even grocery shopping. I used to be upset about these accusations, but Michael was only salving his own guilty conscience as he was the one having the affairs.

My mother used to say to me, "Can't you see what he is doing to you," but you know, I couldn't at that time. However, as the years went by I did start to realise what he was doing and bit by bit took more and more of my power back. I really was a work-in-progress and this of course, caused some huge emotional arguments. But I wouldn't give in if I wanted to do something. Can you see now how I was conditioned for most of my life from that event that happened to me when I was eight years old? I had no self-confidence or self-esteem.

As my children were growing up, of course like any family, you have your issues and problems. I later worked through these bit by bit, with each child, whereas at the time I felt my heart was being broken with each one. I didn't have any help in these family situations as Michael's mind space was so different to mine. I was by myself in trying to make the right decisions because at the time I didn't have the understanding I now have. My children were each having their own experience of life, as was I.

At one stage, there was a time when the boys were engaged and close to being married; Jenny was finishing high school and there were quite a few family issues going on. I was in the middle of menopause and having a hard time and along with the constant criticism from Michael, I felt that I just wanted out of it all. I didn't want to be here anymore.

One weekend when Michael went fishing, Jenny was at a friend's place and the boys away, I thought, *Great, now I can do it*. I had some pills, plus some of Michael's and on a Saturday afternoon I went to bed, closed all the blinds and curtains and decided I was going to end it all. I was in a very unhappy state of mind. I had let my energy become very low and I was thinking, *They won't find me till late Sunday*. I felt helpless at this time, with no support from my husband and also felt alienated from my children. I never talked to them about what was really happening between their father and myself as I was trying to protect them.

As I lay there, I saw a spot of light on the wall opposite me. I watched it grow larger and larger, so big it began to swirl, filling the whole wall. I was fascinated as it continued all around the walls till I was surrounded and the whole room was filled with golden light. I forgot all about taking the pills that were sitting on the bedside table.

I fell asleep and slept all night and when I woke up all those suicidal feelings had gone and were replaced by a wonderful feeling of love. I had the realisation that I wasn't meant to go and as I was still in a stage of "waking up" to what life was all about, I then understood and made the choice that suicide was not the way to solve my problems. I just had to face it, be strong and stay in my power as best I could and not let myself become the victim of my circumstance.

I was saved from myself again and I never contemplated that measure ever again, but I can certainly understand anyone who may think that way. Since then, I have a greater understanding and I know it isn't the way to go as it only lowers your vibrational level and low vibrations attract low energies which is not the way to set yourself free. Also my real purpose in life hadn't been realised yet and I felt this was all part of my life's plan that I had to go through, a test really to see if I had the power to get myself out of that situation.

I told myself, "You've never been a quitter; don't start now." I have always had an inner engine within me that has taken quite a few hard knocks along the roller coaster of life, many lows—and true not that many highs—but as I awakened to Spirit more and more, I realised my inner power was trying to break free and awaken me a little bit more.

It has been quite a few years now and I have lovingly released everything that I was holding onto with my children. I well and truly have cut the apron strings, let them experience their own pathways of life, make their own choices and learn by them as have I.

I realised that as a mother, I wanted to protect my children from having a life like mine. I wanted the best for them as any mother would have. By lovingly detaching my emotions from them, I left them free to experience their own pathways, make their own choices and learn from them—while taking responsibility for their own actions. This does not mean I don't love them; I love them even more. I just let go of the fear factor of what they might do or what might happen to them or what if I might lose them. I let all that go as I found out that fear and love cannot exist in the same time space. If I was in fear for my children, I couldn't be in love for them, so I let that fear go and let love reign.

I do not interfere in their lives or decisions. I am there for them when needed as they were there for me when I had my out-of-this-world experience. I let them take responsibility for their own actions.

As the years rolled on, many times an inner voice would say things to me; most times I would ignore it, but when I started taking my power back, I would listen and make my own choice about an issue. I found I was comforted by talking to my Higher Self.

When the boys had all married and Jennifer had started nursing and we had moved to Queensland, I said to Michael, "Now there's only us; let's join the bowls club and do some things together." He informed me he had no intention of doing anything with me! So I joined the local bowls club myself and at every opportunity I played lawn bowls. I loved it and as I was always a sporty person, I played even when I didn't want to just to get away from him. It gave me freedom, even though I copped it when I came home.

I became a champion bowler and won many tournaments, but he never once came to see me play or let me talk about a big win. He loved to take the pleasure away from the event, but by this time, I didn't care. I had come to accept him as he really was and understood that the only person I could change was myself together with how I looked at our life. So I went about making my own life without worrying about what he would or wouldn't say. After all, in my eyes, it didn't matter what I did or said, he would find fault.

I'm only writing this to let you know what sort of life *I let myself have* and looking back, it has taught me so much. All that emotional pain I carried for all those years has taught me and made me understand so much about the choices I can make. My God, Michael was a great teacher; pity it took me so long to learn.

The thing is, I let it happen. I let him do those things to me, poor me, the victim—no one's fault but my own. I made the choice to put up with him, but when I had the full understanding that there are always choices and woke up to that fact, I made the choice that I wasn't going to take it anymore. I finally took responsibility for my own actions. Making the right choices raises your vibrations, you take back your power, you don't care what verbal abuse or anything else someone throws at you. I would just agree with everything he said, no reaction to any accusation; then, I would just walk away.

I really do thank Michael for that life for it taught me to never give my power away. *I would be the stronger force, not the weaker force.* I now realise we were meant to be together in this life for me to learn and understand this experience with him and also the situation with my father. Thank God I have balanced and worked out both these experiences in this lifetime and I know Michael has now learned from me as well.

When Jennifer finished her nursing with three other girls, they decided to go to England to work as private nurses and have a few adventures while they were there. After she had been in England for about two years, she wanted me to go over and see her. Michael wouldn't go, but seeing it was our daughter, I was "allowed" to go. What a wonderful time this was in my up till then mundane life. I flew to Heathrow, was met by my beautiful Jenny who showed me all around London for a few days. We enjoyed a few stage shows and then we flew out to Cairo to start our backpacking adventure. Can you imagine how excited I was going around the pyramids on camels, standing on the same huge stone of the Pyramid of Cheops where my father stood all those years ago in the war. The bazaars, the museum, the people; they were all so exotic and exciting.

We travelled up to Luxor, a fifteen hour train trip and stopped in a little hotel to go off and explore all the wonders. We visited Luxor Palace, Karnak Temple, the Valley of the Kings and Queens and then went sailing on a felucca on the River Nile at sunset. I felt so at home, I just knew this place. I had been here before in many past lives as the surroundings were so familiar to me. We continued on to Aswan, Hurghada on the Red Sea and snorkelled around the coral reefs. Next we had an eight hour drive over to Abu Symbel.

After that, it was back to Cairo then over to Morocco followed by climbing the Atlas Mountains on a donkey to wonderful exotic Marrakech. We toured around the Greek Islands, then up to Athens, over to Italy on a beautiful ferry and stayed with friends just out of Rome at Torrice. Venice was next, then Switzerland and onto Paris; beautiful Paris.

In Paris, we walked everywhere and caught the metro to the Louvre; we just loved it all. One day as we came out of a little book shop, I looked up and there in front of me was a huge brass plaque with Rue Roger de Lisle on it. I couldn't believe my eyes! This avenue was named after my ancestor who had composed the French National Anthem—the *Marseillaise*. Jen took a photo with me standing beneath it to show my mother as this was a couple of years before she died. Her maiden name was de Lisle. We were meant to see this as out of all of Paris, we found that avenue even though we didn't know one existed!

From Paris, it was back to England where we hired a car and travelled all over the English counties enjoying the countryside. Next it was on to Scotland—what a magical land. From there we returned to London and Jen's farewell to me after several months of all this wonderful backpacking was to see *Phantom of the Opera*, with a lovely dinner afterwards.

The next day when Jenny took me to Heathrow International Airport to fly back home, I said to her, "How am I ever going to go back to my old life with your father? My world and the way I look at it after all these past months, the people I have met, the places I have seen and the time I have spent with you has changed me. It has opened me up from the narrow visioned life I have let myself have by living with your father and his controlling ways. I don't know Jen, if I will cope with it all now as I feel so free and happy." She said, "Mum, I understand, just do your best and don't let him get to you. I love you and thank you for this lovely time we have had together." I replied, "Thank you darling Jen, for the wonderful adventure as it just reinforced our close bond."

So back I went with a heavy heart and knew I had some choices to make when I arrived back home. I chose to stay with Michael, but made myself immune as much as I could from his critical ways. I just got on with life, always with the wonderful happy memories of my time with Jenny and our trip together.

IV
Love and Fear Cannot Exist in the Same Time Space

—Mark Bootle

When I came home from bowls one day, I found Michael dead in the house. This was quite a shock, even though I knew he had a bad heart condition—another reason why I stayed. I had so many emotions flooding through me; remorse for all the sad lost years; guilt because I wasn't there; anger and resentment—they all bubbled to the surface. I had held so much inside me for so many years.

After the funeral, I sat down, put a chair in front of me and pictured him sitting there. I absolutely vented everything that I felt about him. I ranted and raved about how much I hated and loathed him for about an hour. I howled and screamed like a demented woman until I was exhausted and then I went to bed and slept like a baby.

The next day a beautiful calmness came over me and my life played in my head like a movie. I could see myself—the young innocent child reliving what had happened to me. The young woman looking to be loved and thinking I had found it in Michael. I could see my life playing itself out—the joy of my babies' births and watching them grow into loving adults. The sadness of our marriage, seeing Michael as he really was, honest and good, but so insecure within himself that he had to have something to control and at that time, I fitted the bill.

After Michael died, I found I was very lonely with only me in the house as we were together for over forty years and I was used to him being there. I remember crying my eyes out and saying, "I just want someone to love me." I gradually found out this was because I did not love myself, but as I began to understand that, all that feeling left me and I started to take some of my power back.

I let all my anger and resentment flow away and I accepted and understood why that had happened in my life—I learned the most wonderful lesson. It is only me who can change how things are by the way I look at them and by the choices I make in that situation. It took a long time for me to really understand this, but when I did, I was free. Free from all the guilt I felt; free from all the resentment and anger that I had blamed Michael for. I took responsibility for my part in our life together. I now think of Michael only with love; he has been gone for nineteen years.

One night while lying in bed, I felt this beautiful love flow through me. I felt I was expanding outside of myself with this wonderful freeing love. My love flowed to Michael and not to long ago he came to me and told me he loved me. He told me that he loved me and now understood about our life together and he was moving on. I told him I was so happy for him and thanked him for the part he had played in my life and that I loved him. The next morning as I walked into the kitchen, a beautiful Italian crockery liqueur bottle that Michael had loved, fell off the dresser and broke. The liqueur was everywhere. It had the most beautiful aroma like Ambrosia, as it was about fifty years old.

I looked at it and thought, *Wow, we have finished whatever we had to work out this lifetime.* It was amazing. I felt such love for him and thanked him for the experience. After I had cleaned up the liqueur, I found the beautiful bottle had broken into three large pieces, so I put it back together with the help of a friend. The seal is still intact and you wouldn't know the difference, but to me it is a symbol. All the stuff between us held in for so many years—balanced out and now was all put back by love in the form of that bottle. What a joyous occasion.

After this happened I looked long and hard at my life; I wanted to overcome and deal with any issues that kept coming up and that I was still hanging on to. I have gradually detached and worked through so many things, that now, I don't hang onto anything. If something comes up in my life, I now look at it and say to myself, "Well what do you want to do about this? Do you want to go down the path of emotional involvement, or do you want to make the choice of not taking it on and getting upset about it?" I choose not to take it on, to let it go, to just not care. My advice to you now is: don't worry if someone doesn't like you, is nasty to you, or says bad thing about you as you know in your honest self these things are not true. Don't have expectations of anyone, that way you don't get disappointed.

Furthermore, learn not to care as people's perceptions are their own problem, not yours. By doing this in your life, you are so much freer; life is more enjoyable and you raise your vibrations by not letting other people affect you. You stand more in your own power and wake up to the fact there is much much more to this life than being in emotional pain. Some people in this life think the more you suffer the greater the rewards when you die. Wrong. The Universe doesn't work that way; this is just another conditioning we are told about through the generations—mainly through religions.

I was talking to my friend Mark one day and he said to me, "You must understand, you don't own your emotions, they are not yours to keep. The Universe is very generous and will let you have as many of them for as long as you want. *But one day, you have to give them back*. Why not give them back today? You are the silence between your thoughts where as thoughts and feelings are how we create emotions. This means we can go through a whole range of emotions during our life, but whatever we create from them must be balanced out in that circumstance of what we are dealing with. When we understand this, the emotion is released, not only in your body, but it is also balanced out in the Universe."

By not working out your emotional pain together with the circumstances surrounding it, by not balancing it out, you are ensnared into this life of illusion until you *wake up* to the fact. You need to confront your issues, balance out the circumstances of them all otherwise you are still asleep to Who You Really Are.

All of us who have chosen the Earth Experience have been dealt a bad hand of cards; all the odds are against us as everything is designed to keep us asleep to Who We Really Are. This is the Big Test for us to consciously awaken to all the conditionings here that keep us locked in this world of illusion. We need to *wake up* to all of this; actually wake up to how we have been fooled into believing so many false things, created by man, just to keep us under control and in a cycle of incarnations. When we realise and understand Who We Really Are, we can break free from this cycle and then return to the Source. Remember an illusion is something that appears real in a point in time and we are in that point in time. Everything in an illusion can be destroyed, except *one* thing: Your Eternal Consciousness; your Soul.

V
Don't Try to Make Someone Else's Life Your Own

—Mark Bootle

So life continued, as life does. After Michael died many strange things happened in the house. Not long after his death, the smoke alarm would go off for no reason, then stop and go off again. My sewing machine one day started by itself when I wasn't even near it. That was a doozy! In disbelief, I just stood there gaping at it in astonishment. Another time, a little tray of crystals on my bedside table were tossed around everywhere; I would put them back, then they would be everywhere again. I would hear Michael in the house, scraping out a chair, or walking around. Michael always loved his garden and sometimes he would put a lovely hibiscus or orchid on the breakfast bar when he was alive and one morning a flower appeared; a piece from a dried arrangement in the lounge room—I could see where it had been snapped off. Michael had a beautiful orchid house and we had a bountiful vegetable garden, which he had maintained all our married life. The flower garden was a show case and he loved looking after his laying chickens. He also bred Australian parrots for the wildlife centre. He had a great love of all our animals, especially our little mini fox terrier, Penny.

Michael was trying to get in touch with me. I knew he was lost and didn't realise where he was, as he never believed in an afterlife. Even my little dog, Penny, knew he was there; she would stare, turn her little head to the side and bark. I knew I had to do something to help him, so I sat down and pictured him in front of me and said, "Michael I understand, I want you to look around, your mother is there to take you where you are meant to be. Don't be in fear, remember the things I used to say to you about death—open your mind and go with love to where you are meant to be." I felt his energy leave and I didn't hear from him again until years later when he came to tell me he understood and was moving on and our bottle broke.

I have since realised that we go to a vibrational level that corresponds with our own human vibration and this is the Universal Law of Attraction.

Before all this was to happen though, I had had a trip to Germany to stay with friends for a while after Michael died. Jennifer rang me one night to say she was missing me and had come up from Brisbane—where she was nursing—to stay in the house. She said she was asleep in my bed, when she heard her father in the house. This frightened her so she rang her brother Greg, who lived nearby and he came over and told her he had heard him also when he was checking up on the house. She packed up and went back to Brisbane at 3am, a two hour drive away. She said she was saying to herself, "Why am I frightened, Dad never hurt me in life, why would he hurt me in death?"

That's why when I came home from Germany, I knew I had to explain death to him and release him from this dimension. When you go into the next dimension after death, there are many dimensions within that dimension and your vibrational energy, by Law of Attraction, must go to a dimension of similar energy. This is all about your understanding and knowledge of Who You Really Are.

Do *you* ever ask yourself: *Who am I? Why am I here? What is my purpose in life? Why am I with this family and around these friends?*

We have all chosen to be here for experiences in this third dimension and having had these experiences throughout so many various lifetimes, it brings about certain issues regarding ourselves and others. We then tend to cling onto the things we have done or said. Along with the conditioning of how we are brought up and in what religion, this often gives rise to how we feel about ourselves. Guilt, anger, jealousy, envy and control, plus many other lower emotions, follow us in our genetic line DNA, through from our ancestors.

You could be dealing with what happened to your great great-grandmother. For example, she may have been raped and never got over it, never dealt with it in her lifetime. This action can follow through many generations with a descendant going through the same situation until they finally realise and understand what and why that situation occurred. It is only then with that understanding that they can release the energy surrounding the past event. Any circumstance must be dealt with and balanced out for the Universe is always in balance and will bring events into our lives that keep repeating themselves until we deal with them. As in my case.

How many times have you seen a woman choose and marry someone who was just the same as before? She may have been physically abused, but keeps choosing a man who keeps abusing her. Her vibrational level is low, so she attracts that same low level to herself. She doesn't even consciously realise this as the lower vibrational pattern could have been inherited from an ancestor in her genetic line. Her own self-worth is so low, that until she starts to take back her power and says, "I'm not taking this anymore," she will continue in this energetic pattern of attraction.

This woman will think her male partners love her as they tell her so after each beating. How can they love her they have her in fear. When she realises that her partners are not going to change—only she can change herself and how she thinks about the situation. She can then take back her power with the knowledge that she is able to change this pattern in her life. She can then, bit by bit, get back her self-esteem and self-confidence. This is a huge step in understanding that you cannot change anyone else and the way they think, but most important of all is to change *you* and the way *you* think. Don't let anyone take your power away. Ask yourself, "Do you want to be the weaker force, or the stronger force?"

I urge you: Don't be the victim, become the stronger force with your understanding of the situation. When you do this you will attract a higher energy to you and life becomes less difficult as you begin to understand how life really works.

The most important thing to remember in any situation is: *Love never hurts. If you are in emotional pain, you are not in love.*

This happened to an aunt of mine.

VI
Love Cannot be Found Until you are Found

—Mark Bootle

One lovely summer's day, I was having a cup of tea with my friends Mark and Pam at their home. We were discussing vibrational levels and how my aunt's vibrational level was equal to the circumstances in her life; just as my vibrational level had been equal to the circumstances in my own life. That is, until I woke up and realised that I had to balance the negative energy that had created my situation with both my father and my husband Michael.

Mark proceeded to tell me of a mother and grandmother who came to see him and Pam, to help them understand about the death of the mother's eight-year-old daughter who had died two years before, after being hit by a bus. Mark and Pam worked on the mother and as they performed their wonderful way of getting in touch with her Spirit, Mark discovered that the pattern had Alpha'd (started) with the great, great, great-grandmother who refused to acknowledge that she had had a stillborn child. This experience is part of human life, but the great great great great-grandmother refused to reach this understanding of human existence and instead she took on the negative vibration of this event and never resolved it in her lifetime.

As she never resolved it, it was passed on through the genetic line DNA to other members in the families There were many child deaths in these families.

In the next generation down, this was still not resolved, so it passed to the next generation with more child deaths still not resolved. This pattern repeated until it came to the grandmother's and daughter's generation and this is where the mother lost her eight-year-old. The mother however, still did not accept the information she received; she refused to understand it until her daughter appeared and said, "Mum, we have to resolve this; this cannot go on, generation after generation. It must stop here."

The mother still wouldn't accept it, even after she received the information from the daughter, she objected. "It's is too hard, it is just too hard, I can't." Her daughter replied, "You *have* to let me go, you *have* to let me go because this is just part of human existence." The mother pleaded, "I just can't, I just can't." The daughter then insisted, "*You just have to, I did my bit, now you do yours.*" The daughter chided, "I died for this, now all you have to do is let me go and it will be finished."

Only then did the mother start to realise and understand that she "had to let her go" and then the energy would be put back into balance. The mother realised she *could l*et her go and with acceptance and understanding she said goodbye to her daughter; finally releasing that negative flow of energy. For the first time in two years, the mother felt happiness and joy as she now had the total understanding of her daughter's death. The circumstance that was started, Alpha'd was now finished, or Omega'd. The true benefit of the whole circumstance is that the mother came back into total balance. This allowed her to move on with her life and out of her emotional pain and anguish and she also freed her daughter.

After this session this mother hugged and kissed Mark and Pam and said she had been to many doctors, healers and psychologists who all had tried to fix sorrow with sorrow. To them she ultimately said, "I have finally found someone who didn't feel sorry for me and could tell me truthfully; tell me without any negative emotion about this issue with my daughter." She left as a very happy woman, still with the realisation that her daughter was dead, but now with total understanding.

What fixes emotional suffering is the understanding of the circumstance!

Another time, a lady came to see Mark and Pam. She had been raped three times and was suicidal; stricken with emotional pain. Mark tried to talk and explain to her that it was just a circumstance and the Universe was trying to put something back into balance that had been unbalanced in a previous life, or though her genetic line DNA. She couldn't understand that, so then Mark had to go looking for the specific incident that created this unbalance. He made contact with her Spirit and her Spirit told him it was created three lifetimes ago. Her Spirit then took her back and allowed her to see and feel the circumstance that created this issue. Mark noticed a big smile come onto her face and asked why she was smiling. She answered, "Oh my God, if you could only see me, I'm a short, stout oriental soldier with a big sword, raping and plundering a small village so of course I'm going to be raped in this lifetime." With that, all her grief and trauma was released into the ethers.

After this release, she got up and actually skipped down their hallway and over a cup of tea later, Mark mentioned to her on several occasions that she had been raped three times and to this she responded, "It doesn't matter, I don't *care* anymore." So from a state of suicidal tendencies to total understanding, she had removed the price she had paid for the circumstance she had hung onto for so long and had been willing to pay for it with deep emotional pain. Remove the price and there is nothing to pay for the circumstance; it is just an experience.

Many years ago Mark told me that he used to surf up and down the east coast of Australia and one time he was camping in a small bay in North Queensland, where there was great surf, fresh water handy and very few people. One day he noticed two women on the beach and having not seen many people, he went up and spoke to them. He invited them up to his campsite that night for a cup of tea and something to eat, as they too were travelling around to many places. Around the campfire they started talking and told Mark they had just travelled around the world. They told him of the fascinating places they had seen!

Then one of them revealed that she had been raped in India. She said she had been walking down a little alleyway and was grabbed by a big man and dragged to the ground with a knife at her throat. The knife was as sharp as a razor; she felt it on her throat and she couldn't move an inch. Mark asked her, "How did you handle that?" He got the most unexpected reply he could ever imagine, it was the first three words he would always remember and it locked in his brain. She answered, "It was easy. I wasn't going to die for a lousy root." Mark questioned, "What did you do then?" She replied, "I just walked away." Then Mark stated that he knew he was sharing the camp fire with a true Master, even if she didn't realise it. She was actually telling him there was no circumstance big enough to control her. He would always remember those three words. "It was easy." She understood.

Two different rape circumstances: one who understood and one who didn't. But now both understood it was only an experience, it is just the 'Isness' of life. The option to pay with emotional pain is yours.

> We all have the chance to put issues into balance, but normally only a few will be awakened by the circumstances, by the realisation that this can be put back into balance, knowingly, or unknowingly. From the first time you open your eyes in this lifetime, to the last time you shut them in this lifetime, the only thing that can happen to you in this life is a continual flow of the events that are within the human experience. Once you understand it is the "Isness" of life and the *circumstances* of life and you refuse to pay the experiences of life with emotional pain, there is no price to pay. It is just the 'ISNESS' of Life.
>
> —Mark Bootle.

VII

Every Human who has Left a Footprint on Earth is a Hero

—Mark Bootle

You will find in life that things keep coming up that you worry yourself about, sometimes to a point where you seem to lose all reasoning about them. Stop, look at this issue. Think, *Can I change it?* It has already happened, so what can you do about it?

This is where you have a choice. Do you go down the path of worrying yourself sick until you are ill, or do you accept it in your mind that this has happened? Tell yourself, "I can't change it, I am letting this go. I am not going to be in this emotional pain anymore; I just don't care anymore." The minute you start to care you are in emotional pain. You do not realise that by not caring, just how freeing it is, but this is part of your growth in understanding and waking up to the fact of how things are in this dimension called Earth. How you deal with big or small issues while you are here determines what keeps popping up in your life.

This Earth life is a tough assignment. Just think about who or what in this world has never suffered. Although, some have suffered more so than others depending on your level of understanding of this dimension.

One of the most important things to realise in this life is that *you are not your body.* The body is a vehicle for your Consciousness, your vibration or Soul, as some call it in this dimension. So many people do not realise this. Your body truly is a wondrous thing and this is why so many people think this is Who They Really Are. But your body dies; your body is not the real you. The real you is your Eternal Consciousness.

When the body dies, the real you does not. The real you, your Eternal Consciousness, will go to the dimension of your vibrational level; the level matching your understanding of what you have achieved in your past lives and your understanding of the life you just left.

If you choose to come back into another incarnation, you choose another body into which you incarnate so that you are around the people you haven't dealt with both in your previous life and other past lives. It doesn't matter how long it takes; Universal time is no time. Earth has linear time. It may take many more life times for you to wake up and realise what this world of illusion called Earth is really all about, but it doesn't matter how long it takes. After all, you are Eternal.

The most difficult people and the most challenging times in your life, as I have learned, are the greatest gifts given to us to really look at ourselves in a different way, as opposed to how we have been conditioned to deal with life. Have you ever noticed or realised we are bombarded with so much to absorb round us? The news is always so negative: wars, fighting, break-ins, murders, rapes, shootings and youth violence. All of this we hear every day and this puts people into fear. Fear they may lose their house or be broken into, fear of the future, fear of losing someone close to them, fear for the world, fear about everything. This is all a deliberate ploy to keep us in constant fear of what might happen. This fear is your challenge. Your big step forward in your pathway is to understand this test—to realise. Yes—listen to it all, think about it and if you cannot change the situation, step back, send love to it, then release it from your mind. Don't hang onto it as that takes your mind away from remembering Who You Really Are.

For when you remember this, your vibrations stay high. You are informed, but you don't take the negativity on, therefore your vibrations are not lowered to attract lower vibrations to you. If you put this remembrance into practice, when you realise you cannot change a situation and you accept and understand instead; doing this frees you of those negative emotions and stops you continually thinking about something you cannot change.

If something has happened in your past, say a quarrel which caused a separation from someone close to you and it festers inside of you where you cannot stop thinking about it—sit down and stop. Is it an issue being shown to you that needs to be put back into balance? All these circumstances that crop up in our lives are really gifts to show us our strength, let go of these issues and put our bodies back into balance.

Be honest with yourself: What was your part in this? It takes two to quarrel. Can you approach the other person, talk about it, but if it doesn't resolve that way with you taking responsibility for your part in it, then stop punishing yourself. You have the knowledge of your part in it, so change the way you think about it, let it go and free yourself of your self-imposed emotional chains. You have taken responsibility so now let it go, there is nothing to forgive. This may be a situation that happened over many lifetimes through genetic memory DNA and it is your chance to free yourself of the restricting emotional pain. When you do release this and free your mind, your cells will be filled with light where the black spot was. This is where the love comes from within to release both yourself and the other person. You cannot change the way they think, only you can change the way you think.

What huge steps you will have taken in your acceptance and understanding, as by sending love to the other person, it will release both of you from that situation. It will be up to the other person to make choices to deal with their issues as we can only deal with our own.

Once you start doing this in your everyday life with different issues that pop up from time to time, stop and think, *How do I want to deal with this? Do I want to take it on and care about it?* I urge you to think, *No, it doesn't matter.*

We have been so conditioned to act and think in a certain way about almost everything in our lives. But, who says these conditionings are right? These are man-made rules to keep us under control; we are taught to turn the other cheek over many issues. *Wake up*, do you realise that that is how we are kept under control, as by following these conditions you give your power away; you remain in the illusion of life. *One Woman's Miracle: Everyone's Journey* shows you how to stand in your power. If you look at the history of the world it certainly hasn't helped by *turning the other cheek*. By giving away our power, we, the masses, have always been dominated. We are controlled more today than ever before, until gradually we have had so much of our so-called freedom whittled away by ridiculous laws.

Freedom of speech is way in the past. If you speak up now you are either ridiculed, accused of being a racist or jailed. There seems to be a negative power that wishes to control us all. Just realise this and become aware that most of the things we see on television or hear on the radio is all controlled by the same ones. So you only hear what they want you to hear and if someone else has a different opinion they are usually ridiculed, or made to appear foolish—so where is our freedom? We are still the modern-day slaves only the date has changed.

VIII

As I began to love myself, I found that anguish and emotional suffering are only warning signs that I was living against my truth.

—Charlie Chaplin

One of the most important things to remember is *to not take on other people's problems.* You cannot take on other people's pain, you create your own pain from the situation that you have created and you mistake your own pain as their pain.

In the instance that you choose to care about a situation that normally has nothing to do with you, you suffer. I do hope you understand this as it is so important. I so often hear people say, "I feel your pain." Take the example for instance, that someone drops a brick on their foot; do you feel the pain from that brick? *No*, you have created your own pain out of that situation.

Some friend may have lost a child and they are in deep emotional pain; you have not lost that child, but you create your own pain out of the situation.

You cannot take on someone else's emotional pain. Mark helped me to really understand that. Everything I am writing about has happened in my life, except for my aunt's experience.

Also, take the case of someone full of anger over a situation. People say to them, "You have to get rid of that anger." This is not possible, as how can you get rid of something that is a part of you; a part of your personality? There is nothing wrong with anger. What you have to do is realise anger has come up in a situation and it is okay to be angry over this matter. It's what you do with it that counts.

Stop and think, *Do I need to get angry; will it change the situation or make it worse?* Choose to say to yourself, "I recognise I am angry, but I don't need you (anger) to come out just now." Pat your chest and say, "Thank you anger you can go back inside; I choose to deal with this in another way, I choose to keep my vibrations high." This way, you stay in your power; you let the anger go rather than let yourself get out of control and lower your energies (vibrations). You can deal with jealousy, envy, control and all these things and more that crop up continually in life. This way leaves *you* in control of *you* and keeps you on a vibrational high.

By doing this in your life with everything that is thrown at you, by stopping, looking at the situation and then making a choice of how to deal with it, you begin to understand and *wake up* more and more about life. This helps to free yourself of self-imposed emotional pain. By dealing with emotional pain in this way, you are freeing yourself of old conditionings and you begin to feel inner peace and peace of mind; you are happier within yourself, you are living in your power, in your *honest Self.* You are understanding how life really works. You are detaching yourself from issues that really are not worth thinking about.

If you can do this, good for you! Keep yourself aware at all times, as the rewards are great and who doesn't want a happier, peaceful life within themselves? This beautiful higher vibrational energy filling you flows out to all with whom you come in contact and they pick up on this and want to be like you. You will be able to then tell them how you have achieved this wonderful state of being and for the ones ready to listen, you can help them realise and start to *wake up*. How wonderful is that?

In this way you have started to awaken someone else to the conditioning of this *world of illusion*, which is here for us to experience whatever we wish, but also for us to realise we can get out of this same illusion (which seems so real), by releasing and detaching ourselves from our conditionings and beliefs. By keeping our vibrational energies high we can escape the illusion for we will have learned *Who We Really Are and Who You Really Are is not your physical body, but a beautiful Eternal Consciousness. By understanding this you have started out on a new journey of life.*

IX
*Love is Like the Wind,
you Cannot See it,
but you Know That it's There.*

About four years after Michael had died, I moved a few kilometres away into a cosy unit where I still reside today as our old house was really too large for me. Over many years I had often been taken to hospital with severe bowel blockages (that's where I kept all my emotional pain). I had had two previous bowel operations as parts of my small bowel withered in both instants. This was before I understood where my emotional pain was being held and why. These surgical episodes were extremely painful, but I lived my life the best I could; an ordinary life. Apart from family, I had some lovely friends—two groups really—the ones who were awake spiritually and the ones who were not.

I found that as my vibrations and understanding of this life increased, I woke up to so much more. I gradually stepped away from the lower vibration of some of my friends, as I no longer resonated with them. I was thought of as quite strange, as they couldn't understand what was different about me but I knew. Gradually, I let them go with much love to find out for themselves what life was really about. I had explained many things to them, but they just weren't ready to hear. You cannot drill a hole in someone's head and put in some understanding of something until a person is ready to awaken and accept and understand higher teachings. It is like walking a horse to water, but you cannot make it drink. Their time will come when it is right for them to understand, as it comes to all of us although some quicker than others.

I still have my little group of awakened friends and we have some wonderful discussions, usually over dinner each Wednesday night at Mark and Pam's. I have learned and understood so much being in their company. Since my Near Death Experience, so much of what I was told by the Higher Council has been verified by Mark. He has helped me really understand so many other issues, especially since I had my wonderful exquisite Near Death Experience. Many things happened that led up to what transpired for me and looking back I can see how they all fitted together to bring me where I am today. These things helped show me Who I Really Am.

About ten years ago, I went on a trip to Lake Eyre in the centre of Australia. Lake Eyre comprises vast salt lakes that go on for miles and even though we had had years of drought, lots of rain had recently happened at Lake Eyre, so this was a big event to see.

My friend Jeanette and I decided we'd take a look at how everything comes back to life after the rain. So with a bus full of fellow campers, we set off for the Outback, the Never-Never, as we called it when I was a kid. We left from the Sunshine Coast to go to the centre of Australia. It was the middle of winter in July, as going to the Outback is too hot in the summer. We went through little country towns during the day and camped at night. About four days later we reached Marree on the edge of Lake Eyre in South Australia. We had been travelling through the beautiful red desert for days; the red sand covered with white and yellow daisies as far as the eye could see. Seeing this, I began to fall in love with my country all over again.

Huge flocks of pelicans and other birds were there. How do they know to come thousands of miles inland from the ocean? It was like being in another world. We went up in a small plane to fly over the lakes and see Marree Man, which you can only see from the air. Marree Man is a huge outline of an Aboriginal man holding up a huge Nulla Nulla (club).The outline is about nine miles long and three miles wide and no one knows who did it or where it came from, as it is so remote out there. We were camped at Marree that night and after songs and bush poems around the campfire, Jeanette went to bed. I followed shortly after; it was freezing cold and the stars so close you felt you could just pluck them out of the sky. I felt so full of wonder at where I was. I lifted up the flap of the tent so I could just look at the stars and lay down on the camp bed.

As I lay down, I immediately saw beautiful colours gently swirling around in the corner of the tent and then a face appeared side on. I could see he had a turban and a beard and I half sat up to get a closer look. As I did so, he turned and looked at me with big black eyes and my Consciousness flew instantly out of the tent and into a room full of people.

There was a man in a long white robe standing on a small raised platform and I was in front of him looking up into his face. He was young and clean-shaven with black hair. The next thing I knew, I was sitting down at the back of the room with many other people.

He started to talk and told us he was there to inform us about things that were going to happen to the Earth. I remember wriggling in my seat and thinking, *Wow, this is what I want to hear*. He told us that there would be many climate changes as Earth was in a cycle of cleansing herself. These climate changes had already started and would gradually speed up until she had cleansed herself from much negativity, in order to rise to a higher vibration. He said this had happened many times before to the Earth.

He told us not to be in fear of whatever happened as there would come a time where it would be like a time of madness. But he advised us all to remember Who We Really Are and stressed again *to not be in fear*, as all was as it should be.

He stopped talking and looked around and proclaimed, "There is someone here who is going to have something wonderful happen to them" and then he pointed at me. I exclaimed, "*Me?*" Then I felt like I had been hit by an enormous energy of love from his finger. I became huge; filled with this indescribable love. Two people came to me and said there was something they wanted to show me and led me to a room on the side. I was met by a tall white Being who took me into a room—a small room with a sloping ceiling.

I knew I was in a UFO. Two small people, not like us, were at a desk of some kind with lots of lights and instruments. They took no notice of me. I had absolutely no fear of what was happening. The beautiful white Being or entity—I cannot describe him as anything else—he was sort of human, but much, much more than human. He showed me some plaques with geometrical symbols on them. There were quite a few of them, all different sizes—some small, some as big as dinner plates. On the wall behind the little people was a map-type thing that looked like the Universe and a Mayan Calendar which he said was significant. I asked, "Why are you showing me these things?" He replied, "These seals are for the New Earth and you will be part of that." I said, "How?" and he responded, "When the time is right, you will know and understand." I felt this Being was familiar to me.

Then *Pow*, my Consciousness was back on the bunk! I couldn't believe what had just happened and I couldn't stay where I was. I was so full of this beautiful energy. I just walked around that campsite all night in a state of bliss; I don't think my feet touched the ground. Then I just sat gazing at the stars.

As dawn began to break, I went back into the tent and sat on my bunk wishing Jeanette would wake up as I wanted to tell her what had happened to me. She finally woke up and I said to her, "Jeanette, Jeanette, I have to tell you what happened to me last night."

As my friend Gwen was typing this book for me, she came to the page about my experience with the seals. I was reading a book by Tony Bushy called *The Secret in the Bible* and was also reading in the *Book of Thoth* about secrets that were only passed onto the High Priests and Initiates. These secrets then were passed on by word of mouth and were placed on seals so they would not be forgotten. These symbols told the history of mankind, Universal Knowledge and the possibilities for human life. Are these the seals I was shown? I was told the ones I saw were for the New Earth. I was so excited, so I said to Gwen, "This can't be a coincidence, you typing my story and me reading this at the same time. I feel there is a strong connection here."

She held up her arm and said, "Wait a minute, I have to tell you what happened to me. I was up in a room full of people with Jesus and he was telling us all about Earth changes."

It was unbelievable! She was up there too and took the man to be Jesus but I didn't. I don't remember seeing her or her seeing me, but she did remember Him stopping and saying about something wonderful happening to someone. I excitedly exclaimed, "That was me! That was me!"

Well, for days everyone was saying to me, "You look like you've swallowed a light bulb." I was truly lit up and glowing. Even when I returned home that magical feeling stayed with me for weeks. What an adventure!

About two months after I had returned home, one night I found myself back in the same room. This time, there was the lovely lady I had seen as a little girl and she said to me, "There is something we wish to do for you." I went towards her, but was stopped by an invisible wall and felt myself falling very gently backwards while hands helped me to lie down on my back.

I lay there, she came towards me and lovingly said, "Just relax. I'm going to remove some of the darkness." As I lay there, I thought *Darkness! I'm in the wrong place* and tried to get up. Gentle hands held me down. I sent my thoughts out to Jesus and said, "Jesus, I need you" and instantly a beautiful column of gold light was there at my side. I relaxed. I knew I was safe. The lady came behind me, kneeled down and placed one hand at the back of my head near my neck and the other on my forehead. Immediately, I felt completely relaxed. She then did something to the top of my head and I felt a huge release all around the upper levels of my mind; it was quite extraordinary. Then she said to me with so much love, "Darkness is only ignorance of your conditioning in this and other lives, it is time for it to go, darkness is only lacking Light and Light is Love."

Next, they took me back to that room on the side! I was met once again by my beautiful Being and he showed me the seals with the geometrical patterns on them once again .I can only assume that after the darkness was removed, I would have more knowledge about them when the time was right for me to know.

This beautiful experience, along with the one at Lake Eyre started opening up my real understanding of life and what it was all about. I felt like a different person; it was like I had shed the layers of my old Self. My mind expanded and I couldn't go back and think in the old way of how I used to be. I looked at everything differently and saw where I had been so restricted and conditioned in my thinking of how things were. I now had a completely different view of life. This was such a wonderful awakening into Who I Really Am, as are all of us: *A beautiful Consciousness having an Earthly experience, playing an intricate game of rediscovering Who We Really Are!*

I began to have things spoken into my right ear more and more. This had happened to me all my life, but now it was more frequent as my vibrations had risen higher and I was more in tune with myself. More than ever, I found I was relying more on my inner knowing, rather than reaching outside of myself for help. I was really learning to take back and stay in my own power; I was a constant work-in-progress.

A few years later, I went with some friends on a trip around Australia to places I had never been but had always wanted to see. Especially across the Nullarbor Plain to Western Australia, as there are so many beautiful places to see there. We all saw a UFO on the trip across the Nullarbor, as well as a huge ball of light. However, I became ill in Perth and had to fly back home to Queensland as my old bowel trouble was playing up.

I went to see the specialist and was told I had to have an operation. I held out for a year before I went in to have it. I just knew I was going to have a wonderful spiritual experience, my inner voice had told me that. How these experiences work is certainly different to how you think they will! I told all my friends this before I went into the hospital.

In the meantime, before I went to the hospital some things happened to me that after my hospital experience was over, I could look back and realise they fitted together like a jigsaw puzzle.

I went to Brisbane with some friends to attend a seminar held by Wayne Dyer and Doreen Virtue. I had felt strange all day—I nearly didn't go—but seeing I was not driving, I went along with my friends anyway. We were in the huge Brisbane Town Hall; Wayne, a lovely man, came out and shared his wisdom with us with lots of laughs. The energy of the whole place was beautiful. During this time, I still felt so strange, I remember looking to the back and thinking I could go and get some fresh air if need be but it was packed with people and we were down near the front in the middle of a row. However, my inner voice kept saying to me, "You will be alright."

Doreen came out next and her lovely energy spread over us too, as it had with Wayne and I could hear her talking, but she seemed so far away. I said to my friend Heather, "I feel so strange." Then I saw and felt a huge cone shaped thing come whirling over me; I could feel the breeze from it and then it just sucked me up into it. My friends told me later what happened. Heather stood up and shouted out that I had fainted. I disrupted the whole talk!

Wayne and Doreen's husband and others had to pull the seats apart to get me out. I was unconscious, they took me out to the front and called the ambulance. They thought I was dead. I came to when the stretcher was put into the ambulance, after the paramedics had worked on me for quite awhile. I was wringing wet, clammy and violently ill. I was taken to Royal Brisbane hospital and my friend Grace came with me. There they did every test possible and could not find a thing wrong with me.

I was discharged at 3 am. All of my friends were there as they had come up after the seminar to see me. They said Doreen had told them I was going to be alright and she gave them some books and cards for me. What a lovely lady. I thanked them all for their help. I do not remember what happened to me up there but it must have been for some purpose.

About four months before I went to hospital, I went to a Mind, Body, Spirit event in Brisbane with my friend Grace who knew an American Indian there. We were having a chat and she asked him, "Have you a message for us." He looked at her and gave her a message, then he looked at me and surmised, "You are going to have a life extension." I said, "Thanks," but didn't really understand it at the time.

Just after that, I was shopping at the Sunshine Plaza at Maroochydore and I ran into an old friend of my mothers. Mum had passed away years before this. Over a cup of tea, she looked at me and said, "I have a message from your mother. She says to tell you, 'You are going to be taken up and then brought back, do you understand that?" I replied, "I think so," thinking this could be my experience; never dreaming of what it actually would be.

The time came closer for me to go to hospital and the Sunday night before I was due to go in on the Thursday for my operation on Friday, I had dinner with my niece Lisa and her young daughter Courtney, who lived on a property about fifteen minutes away from me. It was a beautiful night in late April, with a little cool nip in the air for autumn.

I left them about 9.30 pm, went down her little road and turned into the street to go home. As I did this a voice in my ear said, "Look up," I did so and way over near where I live, I saw a huge bright light. As I looked, I said to myself, "What's that? Is it a helicopter with a light looking for something?" as it wasn't moving. It wasn't a plane, as I'm not far from an airport but there were no wing lights and this thing wasn't moving. It was just there.

I drove towards it and home, I kept looking at it when I could as there were hills and lots of tall trees but I could catch glimpses of it in between. As I drove towards to it, it was so bright, all I could see was light. When I drove over the bridge of the Maroochy River to turn into the street to take me home and as I passed the tall trees, I couldn't believe my eyes! There in front of me, very low down was a UFO, just sitting there. I was so excited that I drove up to it, got out of the car and looked up at it on about a 45 degree angle. It emitted no noise whatsoever; it was just hovering there. As I looked and took it in, I saw that it had huge oval windows with lights so bright it went into the next window so it was like a huge band of light.

It had red and blue lights going around underneath it and as my eyes adjusted to the light, I saw it was made of an almost dull silver colour and had a top notch on the top of it. I could hardly breathe as I was so excited and was thinking, *Who can I ring?* My niece had just put her daughter to bed so I couldn't ring her, then I thought, *A car will come along, it's a fairly busy road*, but no cars came. It was like I was in another dimension. I don't even remember seeing street lights.

Feeling no fear whatsoever, I spoke out loud to them, "What do you want? Why are you here?" I tried to see inside but the light was too bright. It wasn't huge, I'd say about 40–50 feet across, just hovering there, silent and beautiful. I remained gazing at it, entranced for about 30–40 minutes or so I couldn't really say, as time was irrelevant. Then I said to them, "Well you're not doing anything or telling me anything, I might as well go home. Thank you for showing me you." With that, it took off and flew over Mt Coolum before I could blink. *Wow!*

I hopped in the car and I think I floated home. When I reached home about five minutes away I thought it would be about 10.30pm, but when I looked at the clock it was a quarter-to-twelve. I thought, *My God, they must have taken me up and wiped my memory.*

After all my hospital experiences, I was told one night that, "Yes," I was taken up and they did something to me to help me survive, but seeing none of that had happened yet, that's why I thought nothing had.

About that UFO experience, my friend Thelma lived on the River and was sitting on her balcony that night facing Mt Coolum and she saw my UFO go over the mountain.

X
Have you Ever Asked Yourself, "What is my Purpose in Life"?

The night before I went to hospital my mother came to me. I woke up and she was holding my hands. I said to her, "Are you here to take me home?" and she replied, "I am here to comfort you my darling," then she was gone.

It was also on that night I wrote a letter to each of my children telling them how much I loved them and how proud I was of them; how happy I was to be their mother and other little personal things. The letters were to be opened if I didn't make it. I also wrote a letter to Jen at 5 am and left it near the phone. I had such an overpowering feeling something big was going to happen.

So off I went to the hospital to have my operation with all sorts of preparations for the next day. I had an absolute calmness about me, an inner peace which has been with me ever since. I had a laparotomy as I was not suitable for keyhole surgery. I remember being back in the hospital room with an epidural block and a drip, with my family and friends around me and the physiotherapist taking me for a walk; but I was in a lot of pain.

A young woman, Kacy who shared the room with me was always there with me when my family wasn't able to be there—she would help me. All my family and Jenny who is a nurse, were all concerned for me, so Jen asked Kacy to ring her if need be if she wasn't there. One time, Kacy rang Jenny and told her to come to me. I told Jenny I was in so much pain and I felt like I was having a bowel blockage.

I was delirious and covered with a red rash and Jenny found I had no medication in my epidural. The physiotherapist came in to take me for a walk and Jenny told her to leave me alone. That is the last thing I remember. I was rushed to theatre where the theatre staff were shocked at my condition: dehydrated with a raging temperature. During the second operation, they found my bowel had been cut in my first operation and bowel fluid had been flooding my abdomen for days causing peritonitis and septicaemia. I was later admitted to the Intensive Care Unit(ICU).

This was the start of an epic journey. I was told later that after this operation my body and arms were so swollen that I had no neck. My hands were like hams. My granddaughter Alison, fainted when she saw me. I was on life support but I remember Jenny saying to me that I didn't have a stoma at that time.

However, that operation wasn't successful either, so it was back to theatre again and this time as Jenny told me later, the surgeon told them my bowel was literally falling apart in their hands. Most of my small bowel was removed plus some of the large bowel. I did not know until weeks later that I had a massive open abdomen and a stoma. I was in dire straits just clinging to life and my blood pressure was sky high!

Graham told me they wanted to do a tracheotomy but I shook my head, "No," but I don't remember that. I knew all my family were there on and off. I could feel them hugging me and feel their concern for me. Before the second operation in ICU, I could at times communicate with my family and friends, telling them I had been taken to different places and also told them all about the massive floods that were to come. My niece Lisa reminded me of this when I was writing this book as they did happen not long after I had told my family about them. But, after that second operation in ICU, I was intubated and could no longer talk to them.

I remember one night hearing the nurses talking about me and as I was in a state of being mostly unaware of what was happening to me physically, I became frightened. I remember gesturing wildly for the nurse so he came to me and because I couldn't talk, gave me a piece of paper to write on. I wrote, "I want Graham." They said it was so late at night that they would get him in the morning. I underlined my message so Graham came to me and I wrote to him, "Get me out of here and take me to the real Nambour Hospital." He said to me, "Mum you are in the real hospital, you are in ICU, you are very ill and I will make sure everything is alright. I love you and will be back to see you in the morning." Poor Graham, he still has those notes. I realise now because I was so ill and had woken up more than usual from all the drugs, I really didn't know where I was—as most of the time I was out of my body.

I had so many experiences out of my body, like someone saying in my ear to breathe a certain way to bring me back into my body as I could see myself in front of my body and I had to bring me (my Consciousness) back into it.

Many times I could "read" the energy of nurses looking after me when they were really concerned about me. I could also "read" what my children and friends were thinking, as if I were observing them from a different place, like a third person. I had lost all my fear as I knew what was really happening: I had been told by my voice in my ear.

So many past lives flashed before me. I saw myself as an ancient midwife with a big belt of herbs around my waist, being flung off a cliff because I was thought of as a witch. I realise now why I had been terrified of heights but had balanced out the other energies surrounding that circumstance in this life.

I was also a mother with a big family in Germany and I spoke German to them. This was a privileged life. I was once a warrior riding a big white horse into battle and was killed by a big lance. I had also been an opera singer, singing my heart out on Lake Como. I had thick curly reddish hair. I saw myself as a doctor tending patients in an old fashioned surgery and a Mayan standing at the top of the steps of a pyramid talking to the people. I had had so many different lives in Egypt, some privileged, some not and had also been an Aboriginal who was so close to the Earth. I witnessed so many more lives and they seemed to be happening all at once.

After three weeks or so, the decision was made to turn off my life support, as my children were told I had less than a one percent chance of living, as the stoma had died. It is so strange when you look back, but I had made a Will and a Health Initiative stating that I was not to be kept on life support if there was no hope for me. I had completed these about a month before I went to hospital.

My daughter Jennifer had been with me and I stressed to her not to keep me alive on life support if there was no hope for me. Remember, I knew something was going to happen. Thank you Jen for keeping my wish. I love you for doing that for me and I know how hard it was for you and the boys.

I remember each one of my children saying goodbye to me, Jenny telling me she loved me and that I was dying—which didn't bother me at all as I had no fear of dying. My lovely friends, Sandra, Katie and the other family members also said their goodbyes to me. Then my inner voice in my ear said to me, "Just relax and let go," so I did and I remember coming out of the top of my head like a piece of silk.

I went through some darkness, some greyness and then into a beautiful light. The next thing I knew, I was in a big room with a Council of people sitting on a curved dais all in white robes, a bit like the ancient Greeks or Romans. There were nine of them and some were women. I sat in front of them with a small table in front of me and someone stood to the left of me just behind me. My friend Sandra told me later that she was also there but I don't remember that.

The Being on the right end came over to me and unrolled a scroll onto the table. He looked at me with such love and as I looked at the scroll, there was my life again all in symbols. He pointed to the scroll and said to me, "This is the life you planned, you have achieved many things and overcome many things and now have a greater understanding of your experiences in this life." There was a section at the end and as I looked at it he said, "You chose to accomplish this as well." I remember looking at it and thinking, *Well, if I said I wanted to do that, I had better do it.*

He told me so many things about what our real purpose on Earth really was. He told me, "You are an Eternal Entity, you chose to come to Earth in the third dimension to have experiences here and to realise, understand and remember through those experiences Who You Really Are. To wake up to the fact that through these experiences over many lives, anything that you have created that puts you out of balance with your energies, you must learn to put back into balance and to realise that this world is a *world of illusion. An illusion is something that appears real in a point in time*, but everything that is an *illusion* can be destroyed, except for one thing and that is your Eternal Consciousness, your vibration."

He was so loving as he explained things to me. He said to me, "Love is all, Love and Fear cannot exist in the same time space; if you are in love, you cannot be in Fear." (Mark Bootle also said this to me later on). "Humans are conditioned to fear just about everything in life because that is how we are conditioned to believe; through our parents, friends, societies, religions and also from our ancestors through our DNA genetic memory line."

How I had woken up and realised that these beliefs and fears just keep humans controlled in a box of illusion while they played a very intricate game of finding out Who They Really Are!

I found out in that room that there is no God to judge you, you are that part of the Source that judges yourself. That is what the Council called what we think of as God—the Source. We all are part of the Source, we do not need an intermediary to connect us to the Source, we already have our own connection through our Higher Self.

I saw things in my life I had created and dealt with, but there were no recriminations and that the only so-called Hell you go through is your own, with Hell representing your emotional pain—until you understand the circumstance of that issue and balance out the energies. Everything He said to me was said in Love. I looked at that last bit of my life on that scroll and He gave me a choice whether to complete the final part or not. I looked at it again and thought, *Okay I'll do that.* But, after what happened, after being with the Council I just could not remember what it was I had to do; it was just out of my grasp. I'll tell you later how I found out what it was as I wasn't meant to remember that bit of my life just then.

As soon as I said, "Okay," I was out of the Council and up in a room filled with people with the most beautiful feeling of love everywhere. It was like a Welcome Home Party. I looked around and there by my side was my mother, nanna, aunties, friends, all the people I loved and who had died. I did not see Michael or my father, (they may have been in a different dimension).

My mother hugged and kissed me, everyone gathered around me. I looked to the other side of the room and there were other people there I knew but I couldn't quite place them—except for my Beautiful Lady. Everyone had the most beautiful colours swirling around them: purple, mauve, different shades of blue, gold, white, pinks, green; so many different shades that I was enthralled. I thought to myself, *What colour am I?* I looked down at myself and there was nothing there, only my Consciousness but they could all see me and me them. Everyone was youngish, beautiful and so happy.

My mother looked at me and told me she loved me and smiled her lovely smile. I felt wrapped in Love. Then she said, "Here is someone to see you." I looked and saw a man in a long white robe coming towards me and I remember thinking, *I wonder what he wants to say to me?* He came up to me and I can still see him in my mind's eye. I wish I was an artist to draw his face, he had salt and pepper coloured hair, a beard and moustache, lovely smooth olive coloured skin and he had dark penetrating eyes. He was lovely. If there is a Jesus, I would say it was Him.

He said to me, "Time for you to go back." I replied, "I don't want to." He told me, "You chose to stay." I was shocked and replied, "When did I do that?" Then I remembered. I had done that in the Council room. Next thing I knew I was out of there and looking back, I think that was the time I was being told to breathe a certain way to bring me back into my body; my Spirit body back into my physical body. This Spirit body follows us through each incarnation, not to be confused with the Consciousness as they are two different things. Your Spirit is with you for your human body; your Consciousness is the *real you* for your Source connection.

XI

*When Your Inner Self
Becomes Your Outer Self,
Your Outer Self is Everywhere.*

—Mark Bootle

I was back! I was back in my physical body just lying there with my family all around me. No tubes, no nothing; everything had been taken off me. I have no idea how long I was gone, but my children were hugging and kissing me with tears in their eyes. They didn't tell me what had happened as I was trying to assimilate where I was; everything was so surreal.

My family didn't want to upset me but they had also been through terrible stress and trauma over me for many weeks. I had no idea at that time about my huge open abdomen or stoma. I was put in a room in 1 C ward to die once again, as I later found out my stoma had died and the doctors said I would be gone within twenty-four hours. Jenny told me later after I had recovered that I had the smell of death around me.

My eldest son Michael had rung his daughter Lyndal to tell her I had died and then rang back later to tell her I was alive—barely alive. They had even rung the Funeral Director. After I was put in room 8, so weak and fragile, I felt the heavy density of the Earth so different from the beautiful light energy where I had been most of the time. I remember lying there with my eyes closed and the specialist who had operated on me came in with his resident Jack. They stood at the foot of the bed and the surgeon said, "I thought she would have fallen off the perch by now." He assumed I was asleep, or out of it. I opened my eyes and said to him, "I never want to see you again." He walked out without offering any apology but his resident came back in and apologised to me. I said, "You have nothing to apologise for but I don't want to see him again," and I never have.

All things are meant to be and because of those words being said to me by my first surgeon, I had another doctor assigned to me. When I asked Kath one of the nurses, "Who is Ratna?" She looked at me and said, "Are you getting Ratna to look after you? Well, you are blessed. He is a wonderful man and doctor." How true these words turned out to be. See how we are looked after! Another piece of the jigsaw had fallen into place to help me survive.

After all this had happened, my children went to have a rest as the previous weeks with them constantly being called to the ICU at all hours because of my condition had really affected them. They left me for awhile with my dear friends, Sandra and Katie who sat on each side of the bed holding my hands. I could feel their love and concern. We were in a sort of time space as no one came into the room while the next thing happened.

Katie said, "There is someone here, I'm getting a message, we have to concentrate on the stoma." I didn't know then that I had one, let alone that it was dying. They sat there quietly giving me healing and concentrating then Katie got up and exclaimed, "Look at her forehead; there is a symbol blazing on her forehead." She copied it onto a piece of paper which I don't know what happened to but since recently talking to Katie, I asked her to try and remember what the symbol was.

Sandra said the symbol on my forehead would come and go all the time while I was in the hospital. She explained that it was like three oval intertwining circles with symbols in the middle.

About three years after this happened with the first specialist and Jack his assistant, my daughter Jen was working in theatre at Ipswich Hospital and as she came out the door of the theatre, Jack came out of another. Jack saw Jen and remembered her and said to her, "I am so sorry about your mother, it was a tragedy that you lost her." He had been moved by rotation from Nambour Hospital just after I came down from ICU and thought I had died. Jen said to him, "Mum is doing fine now, it took all told ten months in hospital but she made it and is getting stronger every day." He just couldn't believe I was alive. Jen said she had to convince him I was!

These two beautiful friends stayed with me until the nurses came in and I might add that they were also with me throughout my whole journey in the hospital. Seven months the first time, April through to the end of November; two months the following year in April and May and five months later for one month in August when I was finally sewn up to be whole again. How blessed I am to have such wonderful family and friends as besides Sandra and Katie, I have other friends that have always been there for me and still are.

The doctors kept coming in to see me and I realise now they were expecting me to die. Then Michelle, the stoma specialist nurse with some student nurses came in and said she was going to do my dressing. She was talking to me as though she knew me. I said, "Do I know you?" She smiled at me and replied, "I have been with you for weeks up in ICU." She raised the bed and asked two of the student nurses to hold the sheet up in front of me so I couldn't see what she was doing. I said to her, "I want to see." She looked at me with such compassion and responded gently, "I don't want you to get upset" and I said, "I want to see. It is my body." She then relented, "Alright, if that's what you want, but please don't be upset."

I looked down at myself as she was removing strips of seaweed from my abdomen and I saw with utter astonishment my abdomen or what was left of it, a huge hole with sloping sides where muscle was pushed aside and a stoma high up on my left side. I remember thinking, *This is not me, I must be looking at someone else or having a nightmare*, but it was me! Strangely enough, I still had this almost other-worldly calmness about me though.

Michelle removed the stoma bag and started to pull out all this black bowel—so much of it. I said to her, "That's bowel." Michelle looked at me and exclaimed, "My God, you have pink flesh and bowel here—you are a Miracle. I have never seen this before." She looked right into my face and said, "You are a Miracle." She rang Dr Ratna and he came and looked at it all, then advised "Put her on TPN." (A complete food without waste.)

Michelle fixed the stoma bag back on and started on dressing the massive hole in my abdomen. She placed a big piece of sterile foam, cut out to fit the cavity, then placed a seal all over the top of it and attached me to a twenty-four hour pump which I called Freddie as it was just like hearing a man snoring. I should have called it Michael as it reminded me of him.

As they were expecting me to die again nothing had been done or given to me, apart from pain medication for quite a while. I was so ill, weak and frail and the Urology team kept coming in and saying my kidney function was extremely low. I had massive numbers of blood transfusions and my lung function wasn't good.

I thought to myself, *Okay, this is what's happening, get it straight in your mind and accept and understand what is happening to your body.*

Thankfully Sandra was there and we talked about how I felt as I was slowly losing ground. But, I knew I had to assimilate all that had happened to me as best I could. I would not let myself become a victim of my circumstance.

Sandra took a photo of me and went to see Mark and Pam and they cleared my room and myself of any negativity. Then my inner voice whispered to me, "You *can* do this, keep in your power, take responsibility and understand that everything happens for a reason." I said to Sandra, "Okay, it's okay. I have it right in my head now. I *can* do this. I *will* do this. I *will* get better. I *do* take responsibility for all that has happened."

One night, Jodi my nurse came in to put up the TPN. She looked at me and stated, "I don't like the look of you." I told her I was very sore near my underarm and chest. She continued, "I'm not going to give you this. I'll call the doctor." Thank you Jodi for we found out I had blood clots there and goodness knows what would have happened if she had put it up. I was looked after again!

A psychiatrist came in to talk with me and to see how I was coping. I told her I knew what had happened and that I could cope with it. She called me a very brave, strong woman. Dr Ratna came in and told me I must have another operation quite soon and to gain as much strength as I could.

In addition to my abdomen and stoma, they inserted a PICC line which is a catheter connecting the upper arm to a major vein near the heart to be used to feed the TPN. TPN is a total nutrient for the body and it bypasses the digestive system. The PICC line failed, so a Femoral Line in my groin was inserted to do the same thing as the PICC line. This failed as well as did a Central line in my neck. I was then sent to the theatre to have a Port-a-cath inserted into my chest for the TPN and that went directly via a major vein to my heart. In the six months I was on TPN, I never had a bit of food in my mouth. Imagine not eating for six months! After these six months, I was gradually weaned off TPN as it can start to harm the organs. I also had patches all over my upper arms and back for different medications as wells as a catheter and I was on oxygen.

My kidneys gradually improved thankfully, as I was going to have to start dialysis. I have been left with a bit of trouble with my kidney function, but I manage okay. Some other friends Denise and Karen came in to see me and told me they had held a night of healing for me with all my other friends. How blessed am I to have so many people hold me so dear to their hearts.

XII
You are the Silence Between Your Thoughts

—Mark Bootle

During the weeks before this next operation, I was taken many times to the other side. I was taken to a room just like a hospital theatre with people in blue—well, they seemed all blue. They were all around me, one had a bowl and was sprinkling gold dust flakes into my open abdomen. It had a faint lovely perfume. I asked, "What are you doing?" They replied, "We are killing bacteria and promoting healing." They then pushed me into a big round cylinder thing where I felt waves of energy coursing through me, vibrating through me. I would go to sleep. This happened to me four times, each time with the same people and sometimes they used beautiful green flakes as well.

A voice would tell me to breathe way down into my abdomen as my lungs had been affected as well. This is because everything shuts down when you die.

I woke up early one morning about 2 am, while two nurses and wards men were turning me and just after they left I must have gone back to sleep, but opened my eyes to see my son-in-law Paul sitting in the chair near my bed. He came over to me and kissed me and said, "Go back to sleep, I just want to sit with you for awhile." What a lovely son-in-law. Jenny told me later that he had woken her up and mentioned, "I want to go and sit with your mum." Thank you Paul, I am so happy my Jenny Wren has such a loving husband and Bridget and Niamh (Neve), have such a lovely dad. He's Irish as you may have guessed by the girls' names.

Another morning very early I woke up and my room was filled with a beautiful soft luminous green. I wondered, *Have they put me in another room*? No, I was in mine. The walls, chair, bed and myself were all coloured in this lovely pale green and as I watched, it gradually faded away. How peaceful I felt.

I would also often leave my body, gaze back, look at it and think *Poor thing*, then I would float around my room and along the corridors of the ward looking in on each patient in their room. One night, I stopped above the nurses at their station and heard them discussing me. They were saying I was having a real tough time and that it was really heavy going with all that had to be done for me. But as I was such a lovely lady, they were happy to do anything for me because I never complained about anything. I also heard them say that I wasn't to be resuscitated if anything went wrong.

I remember thinking, *Ah! To not be resuscitated* and I wasn't a bit worried about it. I wasn't in fear of anything that was happening to me. Later on, when that nurse came in I told her what I had heard about the resuscitation and she replied in a shocked voice, "Who told you that?" I said I had heard them talking about me in the office. She replied, "That's too far away." I continued, "I was above them all and heard all they said. Also, thank you for saying I was a lovely lady." She just looked at me and I replied, "Don't worry, it doesn't bother me at all." Why would it after my wonderful experience in ICU knowing *we* never die; only the vehicle, our physical body does.

One night, I was taken out into space with two big beautiful Beings. I could see the Earth, slowly revolving on its axis on a little slant. It was just beautiful; I was in awe. I stated, "That's Mother Earth." They responded, "We want to show you something" and next thing we were closer looking at the North Pole, looking down on Alaska, Canada and America. I could see the top part of Mexico with the other countries curving around the globe. They continued, "Look," then I saw huge volcanoes erupting from the North Pole right down through Alaska, Canada, California and into Mexico with big chunks of land in California falling into the ocean on the west coast and huge waves all along the east coast. I exclaimed, "Look what's happening!" They informed me, *"Do not be in fear."*

Next thing I knew, we were above Australia looking down from Cape York and the Gulf of Carpentaria with the lower states of South Australia, Victoria and southern parts of Western Australia curving around the globe. I could see the top part of Tasmania and New Zealand.

Then I saw a huge eruption like cutting a huge wedge out of the Northern Territory, parts of western Queensland and New South Wales down in the top part of South Australia about where Lake Eyre is. All that land tumbled into the sea that had come down from the gulf. On the east coast all along it were huge waves. I could still see Tasmania, but not New Zealand. I was spellbound and I exclaimed, "Look what's happening to Australia." They repeated, "Australia is not immune you know but do not be in fear." The strange thing was I wasn't in any fear and then next thing I was back in my bed. I don't know what happened to the rest of the world as I was not shown.

Weeks later, Dr Ratna came to me and advised, "We really have to take you to the theatre soon to sew up your abdomen otherwise we will never get the muscles to stretch across and join. I know you are very weak but we must do this." So all my family came in and he explained things to all of us as we were all in my room. He asserted that it was a very serious operation and I could die. After he left I looked at my four loving children: Michael, Greg, Graham and Jennifer and I told them how much I loved them and to always love one another. I thanked them for being there for me and that everything would be alright whatever way things might happen. I was not in fear about it at all.

Before this happened with Dr Ratna, Michelle used to bring in Bill the hospital photographer to take photos of her doing each part of my dressing. He would photograph each procedure until the dressing was done, always with more student nurses watching. Guess what, the great gaping hole in my abdomen is still the model for this procedure in medical lectures. I used to say to Michelle, "Well I always wanted to be a model, never dreaming I'd be this one!" I still have photos of my tummy but they're not the sort of ones you pass around when sharing photos!

XIII
Do You Want to be Powerful or Powerless?

—Mark Bootle

The Sunday before my operation which was scheduled to be on the Tuesday, Jenny, Graham and Greg came into my room at about 11am and declared, "You've been in this bed for so long we're going to take you outside for a little while." I had so many attachments I couldn't see how we could do that but Marjan my nurse explained we could detach the pump for a little while and wheel the TPN along with the wheelchair. So, with a huge amount of effort and help, I was put in a wheel chair. My daughter Jennifer started doing my hair, making me comfortable and fussing over me. Then she handed me a mirror. It was the first time I had seen myself since I had come to the hospital.

I was shocked at my appearance and my hair was completely white; I looked so haggard but it didn't matter as I was too ill to care. So off we went into the lift and I thought, *They want to surprise my son*

Michael, as I knew he was flying back up from the Hunter Valley in New South Wales where he lived to be there for the operation. He had constantly been doing this over the last weeks.

As we reached the ground floor and we were crossing the lobby, I said to Graham, "There are too many people out there, take me back. Don't worry." He answered, "We'll find somewhere and it will be nice for you to have some fresh air." As we moved closer to the front entrance, I looked and saw the whole crowd of people were all my extended family and friends about forty of them and they were all waiting for me. I couldn't believe it, they were all clapping and smiling as they wheeled me outside. I burst into tears seeing all their dear smiling faces.

My lovely kids had arranged this with the nursing staff. Graham has bakeries and there was this lovely party food spread out on all the tables and everyone I hadn't seen as I had limited visitors, came up and gave me hugs and kisses. It was wonderful to see them all. My brother-in-law, Norm announced to everyone, "Now, this is a Good Luck Party, it is not a Farewell Party. We are all here for you and you are going to make it." I must admit when I did see them all I thought it may have been a *Farewell Party*!

How blessed I am to have beautiful people like this in my life, supporting me along the long road back to me becoming me again. Graham was very popular with the staff as he would bring in loads of goodies from his bakeries and they all looked forward to that. I was on my TPN so none of that was for me but everyone enjoyed themselves. By the way, Graham has won many times the Best Meat Pie in Australia as Aussie pies are an icon here. I am very proud of him as I am of all my children.

The day before my operation, Susie another nurse, came in and gave me a little Angel and stuck it on my locker where I could see it. All the nurses who wouldn't be there the next day came in and gave me a hug and kiss and assured me, "I will see you when I come back on duty because you *will* be here." That night, another nurse Lea-Anne came in and sat by my bed and said, "You have come to be very special to us all and I want you to hold this tonight while you sleep as it is full of love and it was my grandmother's." It was pearl Rosary Beads. I looked at her and revealed, "I'm not any religion now." She replied, "It's not the religion, it's the love." I held them all night.

Those beautiful nurses, I called them my Earth Angels, they were so good to me and nothing was too much trouble.

As the theatre staff were wheeling my bed into the corridor the next day to take me for my operation, all the staff came over to me, gave me a hug and kiss and reminded me, "Remember now, we will see you soon." The theatre nurses mentioned, "We've never seen that before," and they replied, "This one's special." As I was being wheeled into theatre after goodbyes to my children, I waved to them wondering if I would see them again on this Earth.

After my operation, *Yes, I lived*! I recovered in ICU for a few days and then was taken back to my room. I was whole, my abdomen all clipped up and my stoma closed. What a momentous occasion, how wonderful to feel more like me again! Dr Ratna was such a lovely compassionate man, he was always there for me and I could talk to him about anything. Sometimes on a Sunday when he was off duty he would come in and see me with his two little boys. One of his residents, Tom also used to come in and we'd have a chat. He said he loved talking to me. One day he mentioned to me, "You know Sylvia, you have a very unique bowel. We really don't know how you are still here." We laughed and I replied, "Well it's nice to be unique about something Tom."

I knew why I was still here. I had chosen to stay and the whole Universe seemed to have turned towards me to help me, regardless of what happened to me. After this operation, I still had the beautiful otherworldly calmness and acceptance about me. I was still on TPN, patches and had more blood transfusions, but I set about getting myself stronger and better.

During this time I started having more out of body experiences: floating around the hospital and looking in on patients. I could see when someone was going to die and watched them leave their body. Sometimes someone would be waiting for them, sometimes not. I was shown more past lives and could see how a circumstance in one life can be passed through many generations till resolved and balanced. It was a most beautiful extraordinary time and it all opened my mind so much more. I began to see more and more the intricate game of life on Earth.

XIV
Have You Ever Asked Yourself: Who Am I?

I knew of and many had also told me of a huge white Being behind my bed. I knew this as I could feel the love energy from it; most called it an Angel. All the staff even called my room The Angel Room.

My recovery was a very slow process. I began to have huge night sweats and I would wake up wringing wet. I would also get freezing cold, then burning hot and also had a low-grade temperature. I had lots of tests to see what was wrong. I could see translucent spots along my incision line. I was with my daughter one day having a little walk and Jen was telling me about how she was hanging washing on the line while Bridget her three-year-old was playing nearby and talking away. Jen asked her who she was talking to and she chattered, "I'm talking to Poppy Mick." Jen exclaimed to me, "Mum, she was talking to Dad!" Bridget was talking to Michael and he had been gone nine years then.

Another time, they were on a picnic when she took her father's hand and went to the left back wheel of their car and said to him, "Flat tyre." He had a look and told her the tyre was nice and fat, it was okay. But, when they arrived home and Paul was unpacking the car he called Jen out and said, "Look, that tyre is flat!"

Just after our chat, I felt something happen within my abdomen and bowel fluid started running everywhere. I had a huge fistula break through near where my belly button used to be. I was rushed back to theatre where they found the mesh holding things together for support had been rejected by my body and had made a huge hole in my bowel. Bowel fluid had once again flooded my abdomen and I was rotting inside. Then it was back to my room with the big abdomen seal and pump once again. I was put on Vancomycin and had constant blood tests and more transfusions. The strange thing was I had no panic or fear, it was like I was observing all this happening from another place.

A few days later, another fistula broke out, then a week later another one, right down low on my abdomen. A bigger seal was used and I had drainage tubes both sides sewn in with drainage bags.

The doctors were hoping the holes would slowly heal so it was a matter of wait-and-see.

My Lovely Lady came to me one night, told me her name was Zarah and revealed to me, "All will be well, keep your vibrations high and *just be*. You are much loved." So that is what I did and no matter what was happening to me physically, I stayed in my high vibration and did not let myself become the victim of my circumstances.

Many of the staff used to say to me, "Why aren't you angry about what has happened to you?" I would reply, "I'm not wasting my energy on anger or blame, the first surgeon did not operate on me with the intention of cutting my bowel, he tried to help me. He could do with a few lessons on bedside manner but I hold no hard feelings against him. Anger only makes you sick and resentful; I am going to win and get better. I take full responsibility for what is happening in my life, for I have created the circumstance for some reason and I am going to balance it out."

At the end of November after seven months in the hospital, I finally went home for a while but still with my big stoma bag and drains. I was very frail but still hanging in there. I had Erin, the Blue Care nurse coming to do my dressing. The housework, washing and meals were all organised as I wanted to go home to my own place. I had to see Dr Ratna every week in outpatients, as it was too much travelling to stay with my daughter because she was two hours away in Brisbane. I had wonderful help from Sandra, my neighbour Jeanette and my family and friends.

As the months went by with my very limited outings, I was still in my higher state of being. I did not let my energy get low even though some days were very hard for me. If I felt my vibration going down, I would stop and say to myself, "Hey wake up, let go of those thoughts and just be. Never feel sorry for yourself." So I would pull myself up, dust myself off and get back into my serene mind space. Then the bad days didn't matter and I kept myself in that higher state of being.

In late March, Dr Ratna wanted me to go back into the hospital for two months, back on TPN again to see if the holes in my bowel would heal without food going through them. I went back to the theatre where he closed the fistula which was very low down in my abdomen where the lower part of the stoma dressing had to stick. It was very painful as my skin was red-raw where the seal would often leak. He commented I was still not in a good enough condition to have them all sewn up at that time. That then left me with two big holes in my abdomen.

The Blue Carer, Erin had to revisit me several times in the one day. Erin was very caring and even when I had to go back to the hospital she would always come and visit me. I'm so thankful for her being there for me.

Life went on like this until August but by this time I was red-raw from the big stoma dressing and bowel fluid burning my skin. It was very uncomfortable and painful. Dr Ratna advised me at that visit, "I think you are strong enough now for me to sew you up. You do not have any life, do you?" I would have jumped off the table and hugged him if I had been able. I felt a massive surge of energy go through me. I exclaimed, "Yes! Yes! Yes! Please do it." A few days later, I was back in the hospital so excited because I knew all would be well. Zarah had told me it was the right time.

So there I was back in hospital in my old room, looked after again by my lovely nurses. As I was wheeled into theatre after a wave and kisses to my children, I was saying to myself, "Goodbye big stoma bag, thank you for your help but time for you to go. It's time for me to be me again."

Dr Ratna came into the pre-op room, took my hands in his and inquired, "Are you ready? Let's do this." I told him I had complete confidence in him, that his hands would be guided and thanked him for all he had done for me over all those months. I had no doubts whatsoever that this operation would be successful as risky as it was.

XV
Have you Ever Asked Yourself: Why am I Here?

After the operation which was a success, I was in ICU recovering for a few days and then it was back to my old room. I don't have a belly button, I have massive scars but *who cares*. The part of the bowel I have left was sewn to the inside of my abdomen. I have seven inches of the small bowel, more than I need to be viable otherwise I would have had to be fed with a peg line into my abdomen.

But you know what? I don't care. I'm alive, I'm whole, I'm happy and contented. I have inner peace, a beautiful family and friends but most important of all, I know Who I Am!

Before I went into hospital, I kept picturing myself whole and very happy, exactly as I was feeling. I could hear all the bluebirds of happiness singing my song.

After nearly a month in hospital to make sure all was well and with farewell hugs and kisses from all the staff whom I met during my time in care, I went and stayed with Denise and Karen to recuperate at

Kilcoy in the countryside. These two friends were always there for me. They took me for lovely rides in the country, cooked special meals for me and just spoilt me. It was so lovely to be free of hospitals. As I lay resting on the bed one day, my mind reflected back over all that had happened to me not only the hospital experiences but my life and the people in it who had played such huge roles in determining who I was today. My mother, father, Michael, my children, my friends and the ones from whom I had learned such important lessons.

I could feel beautiful soft energies flowing through me and such peace, joy and happiness. I felt my heart flow with love and gratitude for them all, all those hard years didn't matter anymore as all was balanced out. I let that happy energy flow over me as I fell fast asleep. Three weeks later, my friend Fay brought me home and stayed for awhile but I was feeling wonderful. How glorious to be whole again—*ME* again. I had lost more than thirty kilos and had muscles hanging in my legs but I was home. I was *ME* again.

Two months later, after I had gained more good health I invited all the doctors and staff who had looked after me in Ward1C to a coffee and pizza night at one of Graham's bakeries as a big *Thank You* for all the wonderful care they had given me during my amazing journey. There were hugs and kisses all round and they told me again what a Miracle I was to still be here. I still see some of the nurses now and again and they just shake their heads and remark, "Look at you, you're unbelievable."

I still saw Ratna every month, then every three months, then every six for a few years until one day I said to him, "Time for me to let go of my security blanket." He looked at me and said, "Do you mean me?" I insisted, "Yes, time for me to be responsible for me." He shook his head and proclaimed, "You are a very strong woman. It has been a pleasure looking after you." He told me I could call him anytime if things went wrong as I had developed some quite large ovarian cysts. He told me to keep them checked by my family doctor as I am too high a risk to have any kind of operation. I don't let that worry me one bit, as I know if anything happens my Consciousness lives on. I'm not in fear about anything. Everything is as it's meant to be and if I go, I go .If I live, I live and make the most of every day I have left in this experience.

It's funny how things happen and as there are no accidents, things are just meant to be. A few years

---

My son Greg recently had an operation for bowel cancer and we asked for Dr Ratna to operate and for him to go into 1C which he did. While in there, I caught up with some of my beautiful nurses who said they would never forget me and held me up as an example to many who were sick. One nurse Jayne said to me, "I was your nurse when you came down from ICU and we nearly lost you so many times. I asked you, 'Do you want to live?' and you said yes and look at you now!"

ago, along with some friends, I went to dinner one night at a little Thai restaurant in Eumundi. The place was up for sale and the owner had books for sale lining every wall all about UFO's. I wandered around looking at them and after my UFO experiences was quite interested. One book just jumped out at me so I bought it.

It was called *Alien Dawn* by Colin Wilson and was about people telling their experiences about being taken up. I was reading it one night and turned the page and someone was talking about being on a table and looking across at three women next to him and they had huge open abdomens and the UFO people were sprinkling gold dust into them.

He questioned, "What are you doing?" They said, "Killing bacteria." I couldn't believe my eyes. I was so excited as it had also happened to someone else. This book was published in 1998. I had no idea it even existed. Then I was given a book called *Destiny of Souls*, by Michael Newton by my friend Jenny Burns and she explained to me, "You will find something interesting in this book."

When I read it, about halfway through there was a drawing of the Council exactly as I remember it. These two books were no coincidence; I was meant to read them. I had long before this verification told my family and friends about my experiences while I was still in the hospital. Also when I had recovered more of my health I had given a few talks to some groups about my Near Death Experiences and when these books came forth I was elated to share that knowledge with them. These books verified what had happened to me. I told them, "Do not fear death, it is part of life, we only go to another dimension, you discard the vehicle but your Consciousness lives on. We do see our loved ones again. *I have done it!*"

Looking back at that time with the Council and the choice they gave me, that choice was my test. I realise now, I didn't *have to* finish that part of my life but I didn't quite have the knowledge then to know that and I gave that bit of power away. I could have said, "*No, I don't have to finish that life.*" Also, when I was up in the other dimension with my mother and that lovely man came and told me it was time for me to go back, I could have said to him, "*No, I won't go back*" and I would have been in all my power; all my realisation and knowledge.

This is where I now know that the wonderful thing *that was going to happen to me* that I was told about at Lake Eyre South Australia, was me realising never ever to give my power away because of conditionings. I felt obligated to finish this life, even though I didn't really want to. The last piece of the jigsaw had clicked into place.

Looking back, the most wonderful thing is really the whole journey that started at Lake Eyre and continued to awaken me throughout all those months in hospital encompassing all that happened to me there. Since then, it has set me on a different pathway of understanding Who I Really Am and that journey continues to this day. What a wondrous gift I was given and I wish to share with you dear reader that you too can experience the joy of inner peace and understanding by choosing to make the right choices in any situation that may occur. By keeping your energies positive, you can make your life more rewarding in every way starting your own journey of self-discovering Who You Really Are.

I now know that last part of my life that I was shown in the Council and couldn't remember was because I could have answered *"No"* to that lovely man who said it was time to go back even though I had said "Yes" to the Council that I would stay. This was another test and when I realised that, I had a huge charge of energy rush through me so I knew at last I had the realisation and knowledge for when I make the next and final trip back home. I will be in full knowledge of what is happening.

The part I couldn't remember about my life after I chose to stay, I now know was to speak my experience to help others realise how we are so conditioned to think we live in a *real world*, when it is only an illusion. *An illusion is something that appears real in a point in time* and we are all in that point in time in this dimension.

Take your power back, WAKE UP and realise Who You Really Are! *Do not be in fear, not only of death but of life.* You can learn to not live in fear by accepting, understanding and dealing with the circumstances by balancing them out without losing your high vibration, regardless of what happens. By lovingly detaching yourselves emotionally from all in this dimension, you can leave this dimension by not taking on other people's woes; loving, helping them and not letting them affect you. This is how you can *free* yourself from the conditionings of this world.

This is now how I live my life. I look at every issue that comes up and ask myself, "What choice do you want to make?" I make the choice of keeping my vibrations high regardless of the circumstance. I have inner peace and happiness. I wouldn't change a thing in my life. I have learned so much from all my circumstances and have balanced out my energies so the right people have come into my life at the right time and I have learned so much from them as I hope they have learned from me.

I feel I must also tell you a few things about the negative side or as I call it the "unenlightened" side, as it is only lacking light and as you know, *Light is Love and Understanding.*

I have had over the last few years several tests of how I live my life and how I keep myself aware. I have a few New Guinea objects from many years ago from a trip there when the boys were quite young as I had two brother-in-laws who lived there. One object was a big wooden spear with the spear part detached but secured with twine which slotted down into the main shaft. One night as I was preparing for bed, I went into the kitchen for a glass of water and as I walked past the spear it was standing in a triangular corner of my dresser and had been there for years.

I had just passed it about six feet away, when I heard a big cracking noise. I turned around and was astonished to see the spear with the main shaft facing up the hallway, the twine thrown right down the hall and the spear part next to the top of the shaft shaping like an axe. It had been broken off and part of the spear was still inserted in the shaft. There was no way this spear could have fallen like that on its own.

I looked at it and immediately thought, *Now, there's a challenge.* I went to bed and about two in the morning I faced my challenge. Something woke me up, my inner voice, then I was hit by a wave of negative energy so fierce I was shaking so fast all over my left side. I knew exactly what it was and I had no fear whatsoever. I tried to speak but my throat was paralysed so I kept saying in my head, "I love you, I love you, I love you," and it gradually stopped.

I went back to sleep but it hit me again so I said in my head again, "I love you, I love you." It went, then not long after hit me again. This time I was vibrating so fast but I did manage to get my voice working and

I told it I loved it. I also told it that darkness was only lack of light and light was Love and I was not afraid of it. It went!

The next day I took the spear pieces over to Mark and Pam's and they tested it for negativity. They found no negativity just that it was a challenge for me to see how I would handle it, to see if I was in fear. I was not. Truly, if I hadn't the knowledge I had, I think I'd have been scared stiff but because I showed no fear whatsoever it didn't affect me.

There have been a few other things happen like having my bed clothes ripped off me, something clawing at my back as well as being choked but I know what's happening and I now have a full voice straight away and know now how to send them away. I always ask when something comes to me if it is for my Higher Good and I immediately get an answer from my inner voice. If it isn't for my Higher Good, off it goes. You have to be on the alert all the time as things happen that want to keep you in the illusion.

On a lighter note, one morning recently as I was waking up, my inner voice said to me, "Get your Vitamin B12 checked." As I had a doctor's appointment that day, when I did go and see him, I asked him, "Could I have it checked?" He questioned, "Why?" I told him I was told to have it done by an inner voice in my ear. He gave me a strange look then gave me the form to have my blood count.

Three days later he rang to say, "Come straight down. You have no Vitamin B12 in your body as you have an intrinsic factor syndrome caused by all your bowel surgery and your body cannot absorb B12." I am now on three-monthly injections. The funny thing was that I was sucking a Vitamin B12 under my tongue every day. When the doctor gave me my injection, he admitted "Well, it looks like your voice was right." I replied, "It's never been wrong yet." I just love my inner voice in my ear!

The main thing to remember is: *Don't be in fear; be the stronger force, not the weaker force.* This keeps your vibrations high and nothing can harm you.

Don't squander your life or let it slip out of your grasp for all the things in life are only experiences of you experiencing yourself and are for you to awaken and gain the knowledge of Who You Really Are.

Every day now my life is filled with love, inner peace, anticipation of what comes next and thankfulness for my life and the beautiful people in it that share it with me. I just live in the "Isness" of it all and remember, *Being in your power is true love of oneself.*

So far I have lived for seventy-eight years this time on the Earth plane and have experienced the full range of emotions from the very low to very high and lots in between. I am so thankful that the time was right for me to *wake up* and learn, experience and understand this Secret of Life.

I sincerely hope dear reader, as I have shown you in this book about my life and after all the emotional circumstances in my experiences, that your circumstances can also all be balanced out by *waking up* to Who You Really Are. By accepting and understanding the circumstances with the knowledge to balance out the energies instead of hanging onto them and being in emotional pain, regardless of what happens.

You Can lead a wonderful life,
Full of love for Self and those all around you.
Inner peace, contentment and happiness can be yours.
I have done it!
If the time is right, so can you!

Good luck to you in your quest in finding and understanding the knowledge that can help you raise your energies as by doing this you *CAN* leave the illusion of this dimension without a return ticket.

"Life is like a banner in the breeze
Flying high, or limp and not seen
If no wind beneath your wings.
Which one do you want to be?
I want to be the one flying high,
I hope you do too."

Don't give your power away to someone else's ideas of what life is supposed to be and most important of all, be your honest self in this experience you are living called Life.

Thank you for sharing my amazing journey.

Sylvia

The Letter I Wrote For Jenny the Morning I Went to Hospital

5.00am, 28 April 2005

Dearest Jen

These are the things to get in touch with when I'm no longer here, just to make things easier for you to deal with. Okay, don't be upset when dealing with it all, just remember I am now where I want to be, even though it means I won't be physically around, believe me, I will be around spiritually. I want to say how wonderful it has been having you for a daughter, you have brought me so much joy and happiness and love. Sure we've had our moments, but that too is part of life and we grow from all experiences. One of the most wonderful things you brought into my life was Bridget, thank you darling for that and to Paul also, I love you all so much. Tell the boys I love them, each in their own way, they have also brought me much happiness and love and taught me much about myself and helped me realise what wonderful men they are.

 I love you all so much, thank you for choosing me to be your mother. Till I see you all again.

Love Mum xxx

The Letter I Found From Jenny a Year After I Finally Arrived Home From Hospital

Dearest Mum

Here I sit consumed with thoughts of you, it is day four following your op and still we hope and pray that all is well. I have just rung and asked for Kacey and asked her to give you my love.

I was holding your Bluebird as I wished you this.

I wish I could be with you, but I think you are slowly improving.

I hope this "prolonged Ileus" resolves itself.

I feel have been a little selfish because I consider my own needs, but then that is how I am and that is who I am.

You tell everyone how wonderful I have been but isn't that how it is supposed to be?

IT HAS BEEN A PLEASURE TO SUPPORT YOU AND HELP YOU TO BE COMFORTABLE AND TO BE YOUR ADVOCATE WHEN I COULD BE.

You have such lovely friends.

They care about you so much which only demonstrates to me what a lovely person you truly must be.

I know you must think "WELL DON'T YOU KNOW THAT ALREADY?"

I know our relationship and I think I am not worthy of you, but I must have thought so at some stage in the plan because here I am.

I am sorry if I have offended any of your friends during this experience.

BIRTH
I never knew,
The pain and love
You were there
I never knew,
The happiness
I never knew,
The joy the pride
Motherhood would bring
But I never knew,
How much you must love me
It wasn't within my realm of understanding
It is now

I truly love you and appreciate who you are as a person, not just as my fantastic, generous, thoughtful, spiritual, divine, beautiful, funny, rude, obsessive, wrack-wrecking, mango loving, bargain hunting, gorgeous, strong, supportive awe inspiring intelligent lovely positive mother.

I love you Mum.

Caring for you has been a pleasure and I am sorry that this has been the only way that I have been able to reciprocate all the care you have lovingly given me all my life.

Love always Jen xxxxx

I'm sorry I have been such a challenge, but it has always been my path and my path has led me to an amazing man and has given us all Bridget.

A Closure Note About the First Surgeon Who Accidently Cut My Bowel and Started This Whole Amazing Journey

This wondrous Universe never fails to amaze me. Nearly ten years after the specialist who operated on and cut my bowel, who said those words about me "falling off the perch" and I said I never wanted to see him again (even though I had worked through all of that and had let it go), the most marvellous thing happened.

A friend who found she had breast cancer asked me to take her to see the specialist who was going to operate on her. Off we went and on the way I asked her who the surgeon was and to my surprise it was the same surgeon who had first operated on me. I couldn't believe it! This man had really changed my whole life. She said, "I know how you feel, but he is the one I have been referred to." I said, "That's okay, I've worked through all of that about him, I just hope he does the right thing by you." When she was called into his office, I stayed in the waiting room, still quite astounded by how quickly this circumstance had presented itself, but feeling quite calm about it all. He then opened his office door and said, "Your friend would like you to come in with her as I explain the procedure."

As I walked up to him, he shook my hand and asked, "Don't I know you?" I said, "Yes, you operated on me nearly ten years ago and accidentally cut my bowel." He sat down and said, "Tell me about it." So I did. I told him of the numerous operations and how I was on life support for weeks and then it was switched off. How I was put in a room to die again and I had asked him to go after he said, "I thought she would have fallen off the perch by now."

He sat back in his chair and looked at me and as we looked into each other's eyes, with no anger, or resentment on my part, he admitted, "I'm so sorry for that." I replied, "Thank you, it has taken you nearly ten years for me to hear you say that, it took years for me to become well again, but I know you tried to help me when you operated. It was your manner and the way you said it, that left a bad impression with me, but thank you. We are here now for my friend and I know you are going to look after her."

He stood up and shook my hand, the energy between us was beautiful and I knew the whole situation had finally been balanced and resolved, more so for him as I could see that it was all still in his memory of all that had happened between us. We had balanced out that whole situation, what a wondrous thing to happen for both of us so unexpectedly, but that is how the Universe works to bring unresolved situations around to be resolved.

Wise Words From My Friend and Healer, Mark Bootle

"You do not know what love is. What you express as your love is actually fear. Power is true love. Love to be used as a powerful thing. You cannot feel love while you are in a negative state. It is truly impossible. You must feel Powerful to feel true love, that is the total state of your natural being. If you do not have control, that means something else must have control, which is not good for the individual concerned.

Do not feel the EMOTION OF LOVE, feel the POWER IN LOVE. POWER CAN BE FOUND IN RECEIVING POWER. It can also be found in giving. It depends on the individual circumstance you find yourself in. Whatever the circumstance, stay in your power. Remember you must be in one or the other. You must either be in power or out of power. If you agree to be neutral, it is your Power to be neutral. If somebody Forces you to be neutral you are out of power, which means you cannot be in a state of true love.

You have come to Earth as a powerful being to enjoy physicality in a physical form. You have allowed the physical body to dictate the terms from a state of powerlessness which does not resonate with your true Self. Your physical body tells your Higher Self what it wishes to experience. You have now made the servant the Master. This is the confusion which is the beginning of all suffering.

For example; you allow other bodies to tell your body how it should feel, it must obey the rules. If your body sticks to the rules and your Higher Self rejects these rules (usually man-made to control) it goes into depression or confusion for it cannot express its true nature. In other words, you have lost the power to express who you truly are. Let your Higher Self dictate to the body. Then your body can express who you truly are, releasing all the energies that have been locked up in suppression, revealing who you truly are—a great, powerful, free loving expression of Consciousness."

—Mark Bootle

"Do not ask for forgiveness, for the answer is no. For you to ask for forgiveness is for you to say you have wronged. For when you know that in reality there is truly no right and there is truly no wrong, for these are only perspectives of your thought patterns for this illusion. So in reality you can only experience 'what is' only an experience. So do not ask for forgiveness for you have never wronged."

—Mark Bootle

"What have you been doing that does not agree with your true Self?

Reality is where you put yourself.

Love is where you find it. You find it in Love.

Don't try and make someone else's love or life yours.

You have your own life and your own love.

This is your Personal Responsibility.

Love cannot be found until you are found.

Do not look at yourself with tears in your eyes for you only see a blurred reality. Wait for the tears to subside and be proud of what you see and then others can see the reflections of themselves in you.

The answers are to be found in reflections when everybody reflects back to you what you want to see in yourself.

When your inner Self becomes your other Self, your outer Self is everywhere.

You can find inner peace in vastness, for your outer Self is vastness.

You are now complete.

Be proud of your Reflection for this will surely dry all tears."

—Mark Bootle

Glossary of Terms:

PICC Line: A PICC Line peripherally inserted central catheter is inserted in the upper arm and advanced to a large chest vein near the heart to obtain intravenous access for TPN nutrition and other treatments, for example; antibiotics.

Femoral Line: a Femoral Line is a venous catheterisation and a rapid way to obtain intravenous access to administer infusions.

Central Line (CVC): A central line is a catheter placed into a large vein in the neck (internal jugular vein) to administer medication or fluids, obtain blood and directly obtain cardiovascular measurements, i.e.; central venous pressure.

Port-a-cath: A Port-a-cath is a small medical appliance that is installed beneath the skin in the upper chest just below the clavicle collar bone and is used as the main form of a central venous device to administer medications or fluids. It is a power port (Power injectable for example) TPN, taking blood samples etc.

TPN: is Total Parenteral Nutrition and is a way of supplying all nutritional needs to the body, bypassing the digestive system and dripping nutrient solution directly into a vein.

Vac Pump: Vacuum-assisted closure to help heal wounds with topical negative pressure.

Laparotomy: Is a surgical procedure involving a large incision through the abdominal wall to gain access to the abdominal cavity.

Stoma-Colostomy: An operation to form an opening from the colon onto the surface of the body for emptying the bowel.

Epidural: An injection into the small of the back to inject anaesthetic to deaden nerves for pain relief.

Bibliography

Bootle, M, *Unpublished personal reflections and writings.*

Bushby, T 2005, *The secret in the bible,* Joshua Books, Queensland. Australia

Newton, M 2006, Destiny *of souls,* Llewellyn Publications, USA.

Wilson, C 1998, *Alien Dawn,* Virgin Publishing, London. UK

Acknowledgments

There are many wonderful people I wish to thank who have made my life so much richer by their love, compassion, understanding, expertise and downright plain help when needed.

I thank them all with heartfelt love and thank The Powers That Be that they are all in my life for a purpose.

My loving children and families.

Michael, Lyndal and Jason.

Greg, Graham, Rhonda, Alison and Ricky.

Jennifer, Paul, Bridget and Niamh.

My dear niece Lisa, Norm and Courtney.

My spiritual daughter Briena Robson.

To my dear friends Sandra Andrews and Katie Perrett.

You and I know what you did for me.

Other dear friends who have helped me on the long road back.

Marilyn Bellamy and Bill Morgan, thank you for the help with my book.

Gwen Hodder, thank you for helping me put my book together, I just couldn't have done it without you. You are such a wonderful help.

Thanks, Jeanette Payne—everyone should have a neighbour like you.

To Mark Bootle and Pam Lahy, many thanks for helping me put all the pieces together.

To Craig Stanley, my hairdresser who cut my hair for all those long months in the hospital. (He hates hospitals.)

To all my other dear friends who helped me along the way with visits, flowers, healings and happy smiles.

Heather and Rod Vince, Fay Derby, Esther and Phil Toranto, Jenny Burns, Denise Bradshaw, Karen and Jeffrey Salisbury,

Gillian Clements, David and Lyn Rose,. Jo Smith, Wendy Maher, Graham Beetham.

John Hartley, thank you John for your invaluable help with this book.

Four other friends Meryl Morey, Thelma Rogers, Alma Lane and Jess Hartley now enjoying the Great Beyond.

Last but not least, Dr Ratna Asneervatham and his team. This wonderful doctor saved my life, he is truly living his life's purpose, thank you Ratna.

Mark and his band of Earth Angel nurses in IC Ward Nambour General Hospital who nursed me with such compassion all those long months.

Thank you to all the ICU staff of Nambour General Hospital for all your wonderful care

Someone was certainly looking after me when you all came into my life, saved me and helped me to be Who I Am Today. I hold you all *dear to my heart*.

Thank You.

Printed in Great Britain
by Amazon